The JOY of STRESS

by Peter G. Hanson, M.D.

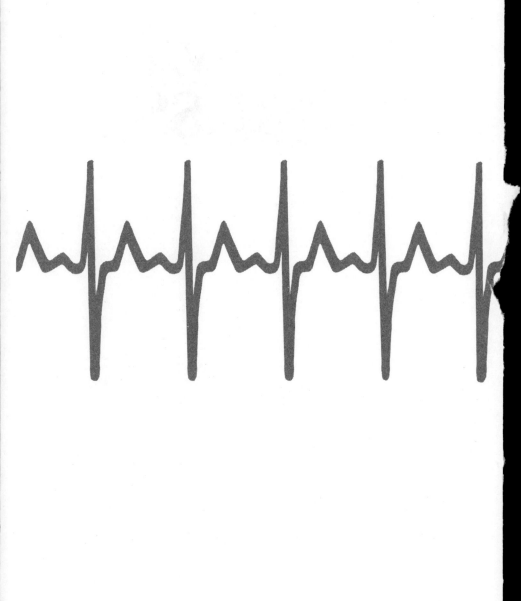

The JOYof STRESS

by Peter G. Hanson, M.D.

Hanson Stress Management Organization

Canadian Cataloguing in Publication Data

Hanson, Peter G. (Peter George), 1947–
    The joy of stress

Bibliography: p.
Includes index.
ISBN 0-9691879-2-0

1. Stress (Psychology).   2. Stress (Physiology).
3. Health.   I. Hanson Stress Management
Organization (Islington, Ont.)   II. Title.

BF575.S75H36   1985   158'.1   C84-099758-2

Printed in U.S.A.

Designed and illustrated by Barrie Maguire

To my wife Sharilyn,
for her expert advice
in matters of content and marketing,
for "repping" the books
to all those bookstores,
and for supporting me
even to the extent of mortgaging
our home to self-publish this book.

To our three children
Kimberley, Trevor and Kelly,
now aged 10, 8 and 3
for giving us the added
incentive to succeed.

Contents

Foreword

by Sir Edmund Hillary, K.B.E., conquerer of Mount Everest

All my life I have been attracted to adventure—
Mount Everest, overland to the South Pole,
driving jet boats up the lengths of the Ganges
River, and a multitude of other challenges.
There has always been an element of danger—
but if there hadn't been, I doubt if I would have
gone to the trouble. Danger is stimulating and
makes the effort worthwhile. So in a way, I have
enjoyed stress, and life would have been rather
boring without it. In reading *The Joy of Stress,*

Dr. Hanson and Sir Edmund Hillary share a humorous moment in the author's backyard.

I was relieved to find that my involvement in stress has probably been to my medical benefit.

Peter Hanson's approach to stress is very different. It is refreshing, positive, and practical. If I had the courage to try myself against all his recommended plans, I would probably fail miserably. But I have the feeling that his program for managing stress will enable most people to live a happier and longer life and they'll be a little more successful, too.

In the years I have known Peter as a friend, I have noticed that he practices what he preaches. Peter is quite a "goer," who seems to thrive on stress. As a busy family doctor, entertaining public speaker, author, publisher, and fund raiser, he always tries to achieve excellence. Yet he still finds time for his young family and for energetic sporting and musical relaxation.

Peter believes it is far better to actively master the stresses in one's life than to be oppressed by them. His principles can help all of us to be successful and still enjoy life to its fullest.

—Sir Edmund Hillary

Preface

In this age of open heart surgery and laser therapy, you would think maximum life expectancies would be rising dramatically. They are not. In spite of our "high tech" miracle cures, most of our elderly today die at about the same ages they would have died a hundred years ago, when medicine was very primitive. What are we doing wrong?

For one thing, we tend to think that good health and a long life are acquired *passively* (that is, we can ignore our health until something "breaks" and then leave the rescue up to the doctors). However, in fact, they demand *active* participation as individuals. Secondly, we face complex and well-disguised new stresses today. These require a thoughtful, *informed* defense, and can no longer be left to our unthinking reflexes.

As a family practitioner, I see not only what kind of disease each patient has, but what kind of *patient* each *disease* has. When someone falls ill with a heart attack, dies of lung cancer, or simply seems to be catching one virus after another, it is wrong to simply blame "bad luck." A common factor often emerges in these cases of hardship: simple *mismanagement* of their own lives, usually in response to stress.

The easily correctable nature of this mismanagement should not depreciate the reality

of its terrible carnage. Under stress, mis-
managed people do not *feel* at their peak. On
the financial and job levels, they do not *perform*
to the best of their abilities. On the health level,
they are likely to be sick. Ultimately, they are
most likely to die before their time.

In spite of the hundreds of books on stress,
health, accident prevention, nutrition, obesity,
success, and motivation, most people still don't
manage themselves correctly. This is reflected
not only in the death and illness statistics, but in
the quality of people's daily lives, and perhaps
most dramatically in the huge loss of profits to
the business community, estimated to be tens of
billions of dollars annually.

Many books written to date are largely the
result of work by specialists—cardiologists,
medical researchers, nutritionists, and so on.
But most patients still come to their own family
doctors to find out how all this specialized
advice relates to their own circumstances, and
rightly so.

As a family practitioner I am privileged to
have a unique window on the *practical* aspects
of people's lives. I have delivered over one thousand babies and seen over twenty thousand
people in the emergency department. My office
practice is busy. I have over four thousand
patients, and see up to fifty per day—in the
office, in the hospital, and yes, even on house
calls.

As well, I've spoken to thousands of people
in meetings around the world, and discussed
their questions and concerns with them. As in
most family practices, my patients range in age
from newborns to centenarians. Just as an experienced teacher has a fair idea which students

will excel and which will fail, the busy family doctor has insight into which patients will live long, healthy lives. Just as clearly, he or she can spot the ones destined for shortened, less productive lives.

I've given my advice and seen it work consistently if heeded. I've also tilted at a few "windmills" when I knew my advice had fallen on deaf ears. I've seen the grief in the eyes of a young mother when I told her that her husband's sudden chest pain had claimed his life. I've had to console two young children whose parents were gone forever because they didn't fasten their seat belts. I've seen the shocked look on the face of the cancer victim who knew all about the risks of the cigarettes he was smoking, but didn't think they were affecting *him*.

I don't mean to imply that all deaths can be prevented, or—as in the case of childhood cancers—even explained. But a casino can thrive by stacking the odds just a *little* in its favor. You owe it to yourself, and to those who love you, to stack all the odds you can in your own favor. The stakes couldn't be higher; your health, wealth, and happiness depend on it.

It is the objective of this book to help you turn the tables—to do your part in shattering the current life expectancy and productivity statistics. This book will give you *practical* advice that you can put to work immediately and continue to use forever. (Short bursts of well-intentioned enthusiasm followed by regression into a life of bad habits are not the answer.)

Some of the points raised in this book are already known to you. Many others are known by your doctors, and may already have been explained to you. However, there is much here that will be new—in terms of *facts* as well as *perspectives*.

To begin at the beginning, we will review your basic anatomy. Under stress, certain physiological changes take place. Unless you understand these, they could be to your detriment. Second, you must identify and measure the stresses that are facing *you*. Many of them are well hidden. Unless recognized, they cannot be conquered.

Third, you will learn how to rate your own *resistance* to your stresses. Find out if you are "bullet-proof," or a "sitting duck." If you are the latter, you will see how to make ten simple choices to maximize your resistance to the effects of stress.

Next comes a brief consideration of the subject of nutrition: a simple bodily requirement that has spawned an annoying litany of silly to downright dangerous "fad" diets.

We will discuss obesity, and a workable approach to learning to eat *normally*. After seeing all the failures experienced by readers of popular diet books, I realized that a simple solution was necessary. The approach that I recommend is one that can be followed for a lifetime, without hardship, and without having to say goodbye to your favorite foods forever.

Moving on through the book, we review the subject of self-induced stress (Type A behavior). New insights into conquering it are presented.

Are you a success? If not, you will probably shorten your financial horizons and your productive life span. With the help of this book, measure your success in the quadrants of finances, personal life, health, and job. Find out how *you* rate. Learn Hanson's Three Principles to cope with your stresses and pamper yourself at the same time. See how others fail to solve problems by blaming the uncontrollable. See if you can do better, by concentrating on the controllable *truths* behind the excuses.

It is my hope that this book will entertain, teach, and motivate you to achieve a *long* lifetime of prosperity and good health.

Acknowledgments

I would like to thank all those who helped
make this book possible. In particular: Jim
O'Donnell, for getting me started, and Glenn
Miller, for getting me finished; George Hanson,
M.B.E., for his fatherly advice and help in pho-
tocopying manuscripts; my patient secretaries,
Theresa and Faye, and my patient patients;
my editors, Elma Schemenauer and Donna
Martin and the fantastic team at Andrews and
McMeel; and Barrie Maguire for his creative
artwork and layout.

Dr. Norman Vincent Peale, who advised
me to have positive dreams, and then follow
them; the late Dr. Hans Selye, for his inspira-
tional talks; Dr. Bill Vail, president of the
Canadian Medical Association, for his sage
counsel; Laura Ferrier for her advice in promotion; Sir Edmund Hillary, K.B.E., conqueror
of Everest, for his inspiration and advice; and
Dr. Ken Blanchard, for his friendship, guid-
ance, and helpful "One-Minute" tips.

Acknowledgment is also given to the
McGraw-Hill Book Company for permission to
use the General Adaptation Response from *The
Stress of Life* by the late Dr. Hans Selye; to

Acknowledgments

Pergamon Press, Ltd., for permission to use the Holmes-Rahe Social Readjustment Rating Scale; and to Larry Wilson, of the Wilson Learning Corporation, Minneapolis, for permission to use the Social Style Summary and Guideline for Recognition (Appendix A).

Introduction

What's so joyful about stress?

Stress is an individual reaction. A single event, for example speaking to a large audience, can give a positive stress to one person, and a negative stress to another.

Stress can be *fantastic*. Or it can be *fatal*. It's all up to you. As well as respecting the dangers of stress, you can learn to harness its benefits.

Olympic records are not set on the quiet training tracks, but only with the stress of competition—in front of huge crowds. The most efficient work done by a student is often during the stress of facing a deadline for a term paper or exam. The most electric performances don't come out of actors during rehearsals; they occur when the curtain rises before a live audience. The best performance of a trapeze artist will probably be without the safety net.

Serious poker players will play only if significant amounts of money are bet on each hand. With only pennies or toothpicks at stake, the stress of losing is gone, but so too is the intense concentration, the enjoyment of bluffing, and the excitement of winning. Many people with sedate working lives actively seek stress in the form of parachuting, cliff climbing, downhill skiing, horror movies or simply riding a roller coaster. Such stresses bring more joy into their lives.

Too much stress, however, can become a negative force. Let's consider some examples. With the additional worry of an assassination attempt, the Olympic high jumper might not even get off the ground. After a traumatic breakup with his girlfriend, the outstanding student could very well fail his exam due to inability to concentrate. After three weeks of being nit-picked, humiliated, and shrieked at by a lunatic director, even the best actor might have trouble avoiding a substandard performance.

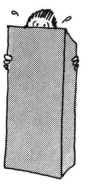

Too little stress can be just as disastrous. The sudden silence gained by retiring from a demanding job into a life of idleness usually causes death or senility within two years, unless new stresses and interests can be found. Some retirees find, to their chagrin, that little tasks they used to do well during a busy working day now take all week to complete. When's more, they often end up being done poorly.

As you can see from the graph, increasing stress serves to increase efficiency toward its maximum. Up to this point, it is correct to use the old adage, "If you want something done, ask a busy person."

However, past the critical line, your efficiency rapidly falls, even to below zero. This means that, with too much stress, you can actually become counterproductive—worse than useless! If you are close to this critical line, then even the addition of a minor task to your hectic schedule (for example, trying first thing Monday morning to find where your dog buried your car keys) could be enough to push you

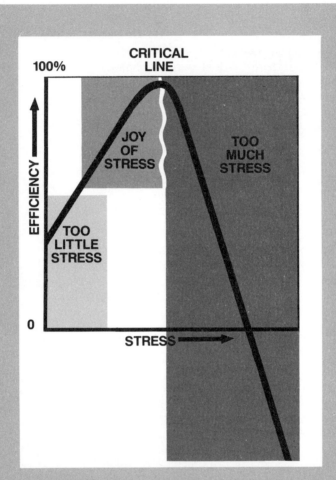

To find where you are on this graph, simply ask one question: "Will the added stress of a new responsibility at work or at home (no matter how small) increase my efficiency, or decrease it?" To make the best use of your energy, make sure your tasks are essential to your health, wealth, and happiness, and not a waste of time.

past your peak. When you are in that state, even things you normally do well will be beyond your grasp.

The graph applies to everyone, but the amounts and kinds of stress needed to reach maximum efficiency are different in each individual. The graph is also dynamic—it changes with every change in your life. Thus you should refer to it frequently.

If you are in the area of too little stress, you should say "yes" to extra duties at home or at work or in your recreation. You could say "yes" to a more expensive house, if you need one, assuming that this is a good investment. Such extra responsibilities will add needed stress, and can improve your overall efficiency (and happiness) dramatically.

If you are in the area of too much stress, part of the solution will be learning how to say "no." In this book I will give you some additional tips on harnessing your own potentials and skills to shore up your defenses. These include: trimming inessential activities such as volunteer work, serving on committees, and even perhaps some maintenance jobs around the house; learning to delegate where possible. If your lifestyle is bankrupting you, come down a peg. Consider moving to a smaller place, selling the frills, and simplifying your life.

To know the Joy of Stress, know thyself. Seek skills that suit your aptitudes during your learning years; and seek activities that use your skills for the rest of your life. Assess your stresses, and then make the right choices to become resistant to them instead of vulnerable. (See the Hanson Scale of Stress Management, Chapter 3.)

Strive to maximize success by investing your energy and time in all four quadrants of your life—*financial* sufficiency, *personal* happiness, sound *health*, and respect on the *job*. (See Chapter 9.)

Once you have mastered these life management skills, you will come to know the true Joy of Stress. As an added bonus, you will extend your *good* years longer than you thought possible and your financial success to new heights. That's all there is to it. You don't need to buy expensive food supplements or throw your money into complicated health schemes.

However . . . it doesn't always come easily. For many of you, making strong choices instead of weak ones will take tremendous courage, at least initially. But after you become used to the strong choices, the weak ones will become less and less attractive.

Why don't most people do it correctly? The answer, unfortunately, is unconscious incompetence, and an ill-concealed hostility to anyone who threatens their sacred "vices." The common view is that the only way to succeed against stress and to achieve longevity is to live a monastic life of dullness, self-denial, and rigid discipline. Not only is this view wrong, it is a strong part of the justification of the wrong lifestyle. Not only do most people perceive *stress* as a negative factor; they perceive *stress management* in a negative way.

They can barely contain a smirk when they read about someone dying while jogging. This seems to justify their sloth, as they butt their cigarettes into their emptied coffee cups.

However, nothing could be more misguided. What I am advocating to each of my patients and to you the reader is to be selfish: get everything you can out of life, for as long as you can. Be spontaneous. Be funny. Eat normal foods. Enjoy a drink of alcohol, beer, or wine if you wish. Run or ride with the wind in your hair. Be proud of your fit body and enjoy each stride with your children and their children.

Continue to learn. Take time to use all your senses to soak up the beauties of color, texture, sound, and smell. Conduct your affairs with integrity. Earn the respect of your peers, the loyalty of your friends, and the love of your children and spouse. Push back the boundaries of senility, and extend your productive prime years as far as you can. This is THE JOY OF STRESS.

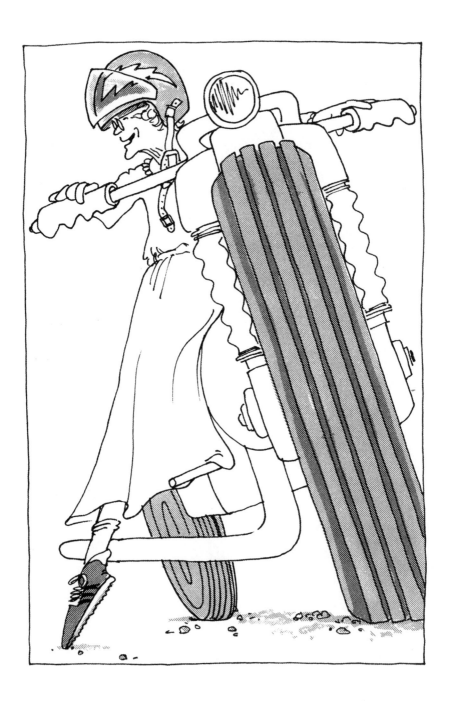

1.
Stress
and
Your Life
Expectancy

*"Me—live well past one hundred?
Why bother?"*

No one wants to die today, but most people say
that they don't want to live to be one hundred
either. Why is this? In our country we have a
terrible image of the stereotypical hundred-
year-old, weak and decrepit, dusted off and
propped up in front of a blazing birthday cake,
and then presumably returned to their green
felt closet. In the last few decades, with the
media emphasis on youth, many of us never
even wanted to reach thirty or forty.

   With today's medical, nutritional, and lifestyle improvements, our current population
should be able to change this stereotyping in
much the same way that Robert Redford and
Jane Fonda changed the image of the 40-year-
old; Joan Collins shattered the menopause

barrier; and George Burns set a new pace for octogenarians.

Most of what we used to accept as normal aging is now known to be simple disuse or misuse of the body. In my practice, I note that the biggest cause of illness and, ultimately, death, is *mismanagement* (which is a polite word for *incompetence*).

As we all know, mismanagement can cause companies to go bankrupt and cars to fall apart prematurely from lack of maintenance. Similarly, it can cause your muscles to feel "old and stiff," your brain to become "senile," your arteries to harden, and your entire body to die prematurely.

Not everyone will live past one hundred, but everyone can certainly strive for his or her maximum "good mileage." No one should die before his time.

In the United States today, there are only about three one-hundred-year-olds per one hundred thousand people. In some other, more primitive parts of the world (such as Abkhasia in Georgia, Russia, and Hunza in Kashmir), there are as many as forty to sixty per one hundred thousand.

Close examination of such societies, which are quite diverse, shows that one common link is that their elderly all have *stress*. They play an active part in the business of their community, both physically and mentally, until the day they die.

If anything, the stresses and responsibilities of the elders in such societies increase with age. If one examines groups of people who live long lives in our own society, the same trend emerges. Symphony conductors, successful

artists, business leaders who don't retire, women in *Who's Who*, nuns, and Mormons all live longer than the average.

The one group conspicuously absent is those who retire into total inactivity, which is all that many people have planned for their "golden years." The whole premise of our old-age homes has been to "protect" our elderly from the stresses of daily life (shopping, traffic, household chores, gardening, and so on). It is now clear that removing such stresses might well be to the *detriment* of the elderly (unless medical problems physically prevent these activities).

Life spans are shortened in groups that generally do not appear to have much control over their stress, for example, firefighters, air traffic controllers, police, and assembly line workers.

The "mythology" of aging

Let's take a closer look at our current "stereotype" of the elderly. Rightly or wrongly, the elderly are assumed (by others and often by themselves) to be:

1. Useless.

Discarded from the work force at the early age of sixty or sixty-five.

2. Inactive sexually.

Made to feel "old and ugly" by the mass media.

3. Sequestered.

Placed in old-age communities such as nursing homes, apartment blocks, and trailer camps, where they have little interaction with a normal cross-section of age groups.

4. Poor.

Due to inadequate fixed pensions and past inflation, the elderly tend to be conspicuously poor. This means they may have to surrender their independence to their families or to society for financial reasons. (Those who have more money can afford to hire help to maintain their homes and independence.)

5. *Senile.*

Once sequestered from the stresses of every-day life, the elderly tend to lack short-term stimulation and memory. Thus they naturally fall back on topics of conversation relating to the "good old days." In fact, the memories that often give elderly people the most stimulation are those that involved a *lot* of stress, both happy and sad, such as weddings, births, wartime, epidemics, the Depression, droughts, blizzards, and floods.

6. *Burned out and depressed.*

Although it seems an unscientific approach, I can usually tell when an old person has given up. It's when he or she voluntarily stops buying new clothes!

Their attitude of depression and impending death seems to render such purchases pointless to them. Such negative thinking, mirrored in the shiny seat of their pants, is a classic signal that life is over. With alarming regularity, people who have given up on themselves in this way follow their depressed attitudes right into the grave.

7. *Shriveled physically.*

Aging does cause destructive changes in the body. It is well known that connective tissues begin to degenerate and elastic tissues lose their resilience. Thinning occurs between the discs of the vertebrae, reducing a person's overall height by as much as an inch. The vocal cords tend to harden, raising the voice from perhaps a C to an E flat. The skin thins and loses elasticity. (This is made much more severe by excessive sun, alcohol, and stress. See Chapter 10.)

Changes in the lenses of the eyes (causing cataracts), thinning of the hair, and a host of related aging signs are well known to us all. By and large, they cannot be prevented. *However, a good deal that is accepted as normal in old age is actually just poor management.*

Muscular wasting is an example. Basically, your muscles don't know what the date on your birth certificate is. They know only whether or not they have been exercised recently. Our stereotypical elderly person has not done any regular physical exercise for decades, or possibly ever.

An exception is obviously seen with those who have resisted the call of industrial urbanization, and continued working on their land. In such people it is quite uncommon to see the degree of muscle wasting that is accepted as "normal" among their urban cousins.

Arthritis is often equated with the elderly, but in fact this disease knows no age boundaries. Many old people have wasting from disuse of muscles; for example, on hands and legs. This makes the joints look correspondingly larger, without their actually being arthritic. Knee joints, if not properly supported by good muscle tone in the thigh muscles, often "rock" with each step and can get puffy and painful. But again this is quite preventable through proper exercising.

Aging research shows that lessening of the immune resistance, mediated by the ever shrinking thymus gland through hormones called *thymosins,* does decrease the elderly person's ability to fight infections and even cancers. Someday we may see a thymosin substitute, to be taken along with vitamins and other supplements, if levels of thymosins in the blood are seen to fall.

Besides mediating the immune resistance, thymosins also release ACTH, which produces cortisone from the adrenal glands. As well, they release beta-endorphin, the "feel good hormone," which imitates morphine in the body. Both of these substances are produced in the hypothalamus of the brain. It is now well documented that their levels fall in the elderly. The complaints of bodily aches that attend the elderly thus do have a real basis and physiology. A couple of hours' work in the garden may well produce, for an elderly person, a lot of real aches and pains that would not have been the case at an earlier age. Modern research is leading the way toward ways of dealing with this. Interestingly, for thousands of years. the ancient art of acupuncture has been used for these symptoms, and is now known to cause the release of ACTH, as well as endorphins into the bloodstream.

According to Hans Selye, every individual is born with a certain amount of *adaptation energy*. It is something like a bag of coins. Once spent, it cannot be replaced. Lord Moran, personal physician to Winston Churchill, in his studies of shell-shocked soldiers, referred to this quality as "courage." Every individual may inherit a different quantity of adaptation energy, or courage. However, once it is gone, burnout occurs. Senility in the elderly and shell-shock in young soldiers are alike in a sense. They both seem to result from having spent all one's adaptation energy.

Women and longevity

Today, most of our elderly tend to be women. The men in their lives, in many cases, have succumbed to wars, higher incidence of smoking and alcohol abuse, and to excess *stress*. This stress has been brought on largely by the "hurry sickness" that attends the twentieth-century production line. (This will be discussed in detail in Chapter 8. Those of you who just flipped ahead to see Chapter 8 have identified yourselves as type A's. You are the very ones who can least afford to skip whole sections of *this* book!)

Women in the past tended to be insulated from the battlefield, from cigarettes (by peer unacceptability of this habit), and from the hurry sickness of assembly lines by their differing role in society. Pressures of child raising, to be sure, are not to be minimized as a source of stress. However, they have generally not involved constant conflict with the time clock.

It would be wrong to assume that women will continue to outlive their men. Before the industrial age, men actually outlived women consistently. This was due to:

1. The high incidence of death among women at childbirth.
2. Men working hard on the land. This meant they had constant physical exercise, but not time-clock pressures. It also meant they had more *control* over their finished product (in this case, food) than the modern assembly line worker.
3. The lower incidence of cigarette smoking.
4. There was no such thing as "idle retirement."

But the pendulum is swinging. Today, women are gaining improved status in the workforce. As a result, they are now fighting the time clock in increasing numbers. Although still restricted from the military battlefronts, they are being given active roles in civilian police work. Cigarette smoking is now as socially "acceptable" for women as for men, and in fact the majority of teenage smokers are female.

Our whole North American economy, including the price of houses, is built upon the expectation that most couples will be bringing in two incomes. Thus women are staying in their careers for longer than ever before. It is still expected that the major task of child raising with its extra pressures will be handled by women, who must thank goodness for the smaller sized families that birth control has permitted.

Working mothers in today's society were brought up at a time when it was less common for women to be working. The belief was instilled in them that they should assume the primary role in child raising. Thus they are often made to feel guilty for doing otherwise. In reality, when both parents are working, it is obvious that the dynamics of the family must change radically from the former model. However, many women are still caught in the middle, with guilt feelings, which add extra stresses.

Thus women today are beginning to fall prey to the same stress-related illnesses as men—evidence that the possession of ovaries is not a guarantee of a longer life. We can no longer assume that tomorrow's young executive who dies of a heart attack will always be a man.

Why not live longer?

Physiologically, based on the number of cell divisions in each organ, the human body should be capable of living to between 100 and 150 years. Anything less should be considered an "early death." True "middle age" should not even start until age sixty!

The example of Winston Churchill is sometimes cited by people defending their own bad habits. Churchill lived to the age of ninety in spite of his smoking, drinking, obesity, and lack of exercise. However, he could well have enjoyed another few decades of useful life. That Winston Churchill lived as long as he did is a tribute to his constitution and to the effects of constant stimulation with stresses. He did not even start his career as prime minister of England until age sixty-six, and was reelected at age seventy-seven.

His resistance to stress was also bolstered by a loving relationship with his wife, and the ability to take efficient cat-naps. (See "How to Take a Power Nap," Chapter 4.)

Obviously, with many of our elderly living only into their mid-seventies, we are doing something wrong. This situation is preventable. Usually premature death results from a lifetime of (often unwitting) mismanagement of health.

Health and stress

It has been estimated that illnesses and accidents related to *stress* account for three-quarters of all time lost from work. Stress is also implicated in the majority of cases seen in the doctor's office, hospital beds, and ultimately the graveyard. In spite of all the media attention to health, stress-related problems take the vast majority of people by *surprise*. They might have known that stress can harm others, but never fully realized what it could do to *them*. Purely uncontrollable (or bad luck) accidents or illnesses leading to death are fortunately rare.

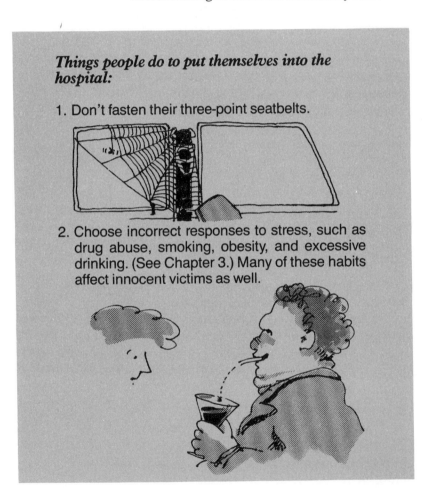

Things people do to put themselves into the hospital:

1. Don't fasten their three-point seatbelts.

2. Choose incorrect responses to stress, such as drug abuse, smoking, obesity, and excessive drinking. (See Chapter 3.) Many of these habits affect innocent victims as well.

3. Fall prey to careless accidents due to their increased error rate. (See Chapter 2.)

4. Undervalue their leisure by working too hard and using valuable down-time inefficiently. (See section on Type A behavior, Chapter 8.)

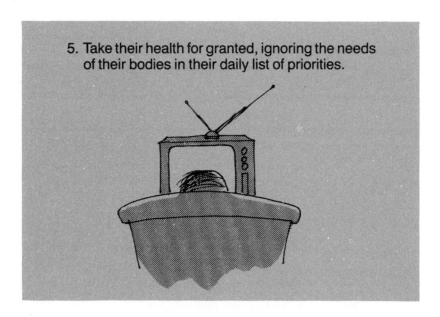

5. Take their health for granted, ignoring the needs of their bodies in their daily list of priorities.

It is at the very time when people are under great stress that their bodies are in the greatest jeopardy. Dr. Hans Selye found that he could cause illness, premature aging, hardening of the arteries, and subsequent early death in his experimental rats by simply stressing them excessively. (For example, he would teach them a trick and then punish them for doing it.) The exact cause of death might not be a major catastrophe such as stomach ulcers, colitis, or heart attacks from stress-induced cholesterol deposits in the arteries. With the predictable and dramatic shrinking of all the lymph glands as well as a decrease in their general immune response, the rats could just as easily die from a minor infection that would advance into a severe pneumonia, septicemia, or meningitis.

So be warned: Something similar can happen to you under your stresses. If you don't learn how to handle stress, you may be unnecessarily courting ill health, illnesses, or even early death.

This has been shown countless times. Following an earthquake in Athens, there was a sharp rise in the number of deaths from heart attacks and other illnesses. Increased deaths, particularly among the elderly, are often seen during spells of extreme heat or cold.

To cite an example from my own practice, I recently saw an eighty-two-year-old woman die of cancer within a few months of the death of her husband. She had had a slow growing cancer in remission for decades, but in the last months it spread like wildfire through her whole body. The true cause of her death was the stress of her husband's death—had he lived, her cancer would quite likely have remained in its containment.

Control

The key to surviving and thriving on stress is *control*.

An interesting piece of research done recently demanded tasks of concentration of two groups of workers. Both groups were exposed to very distracting background noises of machinery, horns honking, and people talking loudly in languages unknown to the workers. One group had a button placed on a desk, so that they could shut off the background noises any time they wanted to. The other group had no such button.

The productivity of the group with the control button was as expected: consistently and remarkably higher than that of those without

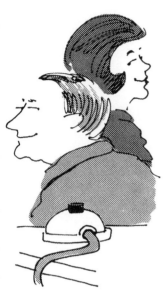

control. The interesting point is that *no one actually pushed the control button.* Just knowing it was there seemed to be enough.

The lesson here is an important one: It is essential to have some "control buttons" in your own life. They help you live satisfactorily with the stresses that are around you. If you have very little sense of control, the stresses will surely get to you.

The media headlines tend to bombard you with spectacular disasters, bad news, and frustrations, all beyond your control. This is likely a commercial recognition of the realities of human nature; most people just love to slow down to see roadside disasters in real life.

As a stress-reducing principle, try to avoid all stories of sensationalized violence in the media, and instead spend your time on the more productive stories.

A good way to handle stress is by the Hanson method: Learn to ignore what you can't control, and learn to control what you can. The amazing fact is that most events in your own life *are* within your control.

Let's begin your defense against stress by learning about your basic anatomy.

■

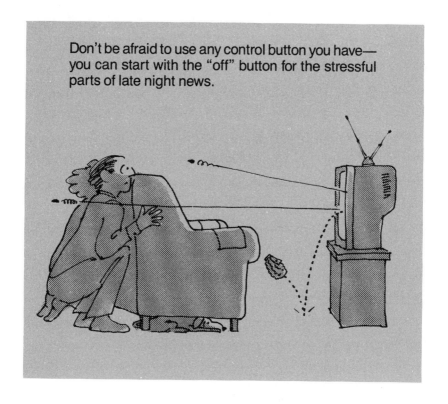

Don't be afraid to use any control button you have—you can start with the "off" button for the stressful parts of late night news.

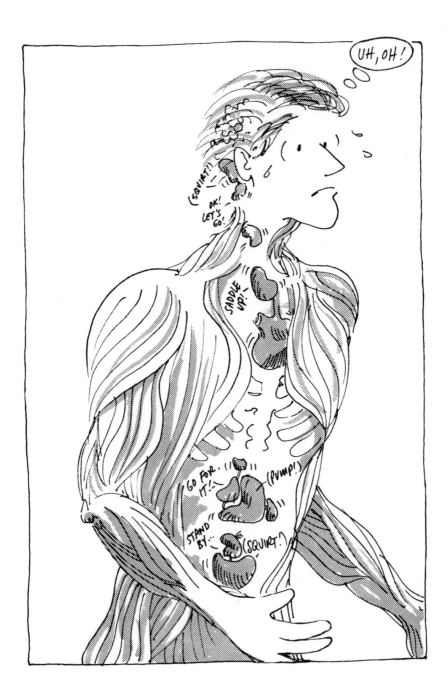

2.
The Anatomy of Stress

Your body as a battleship

Think of your body as a magnificent but out-dated wooden battleship. It has many powerful and intricate weapons to use in response to the "enemy," *stress*. As you read on, you will undoubtedly become quite impressed by your own responses, and the superhuman "fight-or-flight" powers that can be harnessed. For example, a 110-pound woman lifted a tipped tractor far enough off her son's body to allow him to pull free; but without the acute stress she could never summon such strength.

The problem is that many of our battle-ship's weapons are beautifully designed, but for the wrong war. The enemy has greatly changed. Our stress responses were programmed for life in the primitive state, thousands of years before we became "civilized." No longer are our stresses a simple matter of life and death threats; they now involve much more intricate and complex challenges. Stresses such as over-crowding, traffic, pollution, and government red tape were hardly even in existence until the last couple of centuries.

Knowledge of how your body works in the modern context is critical to your ability to fight, conquer, and even *thrive* on stress. Unthinking reflexes must now give way to a *thoughtful defense.*

Stress responses are both physical and psychological

Quite apart from the obvious physical stress responses such as sweating and racing of the heart, there are some important psychological responses to stress. In the Second World War, it was not uncommon for soldiers to sub-consciously "invent" diseases in order to get

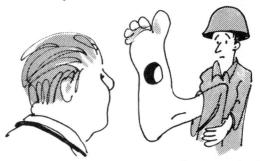

themselves out of active duty. It was noticed that pilots developed pains or other problems relating to their eyes, which would obviously prevent them from flying a plane over enemy territory. Parachutists were noted to suffer psy-chosomatic pains in their feet or ankles. Quite conveniently, these would prevent them from making jumps. We can only speculate as to the nature of the pain suffered by tail-gunners!

In much the same way, our physical responses to stress can be helpful in times of "old-fashioned" danger. In fact, they can even be life-saving, as could be attested by anyone who has found a sudden burst of speed in his or her legs while being chased by an angry dog.

The human body is well set up for high primal stresses. However, it isn't very good at coping with small insidious ones such as forgetting where you put your keys, a single mosquito in your room at night, the dripping of a faucet, or the constant whining of a child. It seems that your body has no sense of humor at all!

Let's take a closer look at some of the body's specific responses to stress, and how the *original benefit* can become *today's drawback* if left to your unthinking reflexes.

Natural responses to stress

1. Cortisone
2. Thyroid
3. Endorphin
4. Sex hormones
5. Digestive tract
6. Sugar and insulin
7. Cholesterol
8. Racing heartbeat
9. Air supply
10. Blood
11. Skin
12. Senses

Natural responses to stress

1. Release of cortisone from the adrenal glands

Original benefit

Protection from an instant allergy reaction (such as asthma or closing of the eyes), from a dust-up with an attacking foe.

Today's drawback

If chronically elevated, cortisone destroys the body's resistance to the stresses of cancer, infection, surgery, and illness. Every lymph gland in the body shrivels up; the immune response weakens. The ability to fight off even minor colds (as well as major illnesses) is greatly impaired.

As a common example, young children are usually brought to their doctors with one infection after another for the first five or six years after starting daycare or school. Partially, this is due to contagious diseases from the other children, but mainly it is due to decreased resistance, from the stress of leaving the womblike comfort of the home for the general brouhaha of the society of their peers. Adults will also notice this phenomenon when in new environments. Teachers suffer frequent colds caught from their pupils during the first five years on the job. Pediatricians, however, have it even worse. They often go through five years of diarrhea while getting their training!

Chronic cortisone elevation also dramatically reduces the stomach's resistance to its own acid, leading to gastric and duodenal ulcers. Farther along the bowels, colitis can be aggravated.

Bones are made more brittle by cortisone. Thus they could fracture much more easily. Blood pressure can be elevated by the retention of sodium, which can also push a borderline heart failure case into trouble. (The common stress response of eating a diet high in fast foods, rich in salt, is thus even more harmful than usual.) Adrenalin is also released by the adrenal glands, and mediates a host of bodily reactions, as we will see.

2. Thyroid hormone increases in the bloodstream

Original benefit

Thyroid hormones speed up the body's metabolism. The body thus burns its fuel faster, to provide extra energy, much as a supercharger helps your car.

Today's drawbacks

Intolerance to heat, shaky nerves to the point of jumpiness, guaranteed weight loss under stress (*if* food intake remains constant), insomnia, and ultimately exhaustion or burnout. While some obese people react to stress by gaining weight, this is only because they actively work at overwhelming their thyroids with extra calories.

3. Release of endorphin from the hypothalamus

Original benefit

Identical to morphine, this is the body's "feel good" hormone. It is a very potent pain killer. Under acute stress the soldier doesn't feel his wounds. The boxer doesn't notice his cuts or broken bones. The mother in labor feels much less of the pain of childbirth than she otherwise would. The marathon runner gets a "second wind" in which the pains lessen. In all of these conditions, the levels of endorphin are elevated as part of the wisdom of the body.

GOTCHA!

Today's drawbacks

Chronic relentless stresses can deplete the levels of endorphin. This has been shown to aggravate migraines, backaches, and even the pains of arthritis (although *not* the actual disease itself).

Acupuncture and T.E.N.S. (transcutaneous electronic nerve stimulation) can be shown to actually increase endorphin levels, and reduce the pains in the above conditions in most cases. Dentists can use these techniques to provide enough of an anesthetic effect for dental work. Veterinarians use acupuncture on injured race horses (thus no trace of drugs shows up in the urine). Injured Olympic athletes are now being treated with T.E.N.S. and acupuncture, because most drugs used can be detected and will cause disqualification. Of course, doctors in China and now in many other countries use the technique to anesthetize some patients for major surgery.

4. Reduction in sex hormones: testosterone in the male; progesterone in the female

(In the male there is the added response of
retraction of the testicles for protection.)

Original benefit

*Decreased fertility. In times of drought, over-
crowding, or decreased food supply in the past,
this was a reasonable response since it reduced
the number of mouths to feed. With soldiers and
hunters away from their mates for long intervals,
a decreased libido made both partners' lives more
bearable, and allowed energies to be focused on
the job at hand, without distraction.*

Today's drawbacks

Usually unrecognized by either partner, a predictable decrease in libido accompanies stress.
This leads to obvious anxieties and failures
when intercourse is attempted. The most common problems are premature ejaculation in the
male, and failure to reach orgasm in the female.
Because couples are often not aware that their
sexual downturns are a physical result of stress,
I have found most transfer their anxieties
inappropriately.

They may start nit-picking at each other, or
develop obsessive-compulsive behavior. They
may develop phobias regarding such conditions
as cancer or heart attacks. Ultimately they may
even seek new partners.

It was well known to doctors several generations ago that an infertile couple could benefit
from a cruise, or trip abroad. Not only would
the opportunities for intercourse increase, but

the actual sperm counts and ovulation rates would benefit from the resurgence of the testosterone and progesterone respectively.

This effect has certainly been well noted by the travel industry, in which the whole tenor of advertising for sun holidays is to make people feel "sexy," to leave their inhibitions and stresses behind them.

5. The shutdown of the entire digestive tract

Original benefit

Blood could be diverted to the muscles, and the "engine room" of the heart and lungs. Thus it would act as a vital "self-transfusion," enabling one to perform superordinary feats of muscular power (for example, as in Olympic competition or in the case of the heroic woman lifting the tractor off her son).

When the digestive tract shuts down, the mouth goes dry, to avoid adding more fluids to the stomach. (Even these fluids will be needed elsewhere.) The stomach and intestines virtually stop their secretions and movements. The rectum (and bladder) tend to empty in order to jettison any excess load prior to battle.

Today's drawbacks

The highly stressed public speaker can't get even enough moisture going in his or her mouth to unstick the tongue from the roof of the mouth, unless he or she uses the glass of water kindly placed on the lectern for just this purpose. The dry mouth phenomenon is so consistent that it has been used as a lie detector test in China. A "line up" of suspects are all forced to take a large spoonful of cooked rice, and then answer questions. All but the guilty one can swallow the rice in order to talk. The guilty party presumably makes a rather muffled confession.

People who eat on the run under stress do themselves a lot of harm by forcing food at high speed into their inactive stomachs. Stomach bloating, nausea, discomfort, cramps, and even diarrhea can result. Swimmers are well aware of this reaction of the stomach. Thus they do not eat heavily immediately prior to the stress of swimming.

The jettisoning effect is another aspect of the shutting down of the digestive tract. The modern valedictorian, of course, is not pleased by the rectum's return to its obsolete ancestral behavior as he or she rises to address the class.

6. Release of sugar into the blood, along with an increase in insulin levels to metabolize it

Original benefit
Quick "short distance" energy supply. Fuel for the sprint.

Today's drawbacks
Diabetes can be aggravated, or even started, by excessive demands on the pancreas for insulin. The stress response of eating an excess of foods high in sugar is thus even more damaging, as the bloodstream already has high levels of sugar as part of its natural response to stress. Hypoglycemia has become a badly overused diag-

nosis (which has given birth to a new generation of lucrative nutrition storefronts in the lay field). Nonetheless, it is a very real condition. Hypoglycemia can result in—and causes—a paradoxical urge to have another quick "sugar fix." This makes life difficult for the pancreas to say the least, not to mention your teeth. (See Chapter 5.)

Consult your doctor if you think you have any symptoms or signs of hypoglycemia.

7. *Increase of cholesterol in the blood, mainly from the liver*

GRRRRR!

Original benefit

Helps to transport "long distance" fuel, now that the stomach has shut down. Takes over where the blood sugar leaves off in supplying energy to the muscles.

Today's drawbacks

On a chronic basis some of this elevated cholesterol can tend to deposit in the blood vessels, including the coronary arteries. It can cause hardening of the arteries (arteriosclerotic heart disease), or even a fatal heart attack. The dietary cholesterol controversy is a big issue on its own, and will be discussed in Chapter 5. One word of caution—if the doctor drawing your blood is a sleepy, overworked, rookie intern who stabs the needle into your bell cord instead of your arm on the first of many attempts, the fright generated can elevate the cholesterol by as much as 40 percent in just a few seconds. (I know, because I was that intern!) An artificially high reading could also be obtained in a doctor's office or lab if you cheated on the fourteen-hour fast requirement (for example, by sneaking a coffee with cream on the way in). Or it could be obtained by eating a very high fat diet for the week prior to the test.

In spite of occasional artificial readings, blood cholesterol studies are still useful. They should be done by your doctor as part of your regular physical examination. In high-risk cases, they should take place at least once a year. High-risks cases would include women on birth control pills. They would also include people with strong family histories of heart disease (even their children should be checked starting at about nine years of age). Thirdly, high-risk cases include anyone who is under excessive stress. (If you are not sure of your stress levels, see Chapters 3 and 4.)

It is clear that the last thing you need to add to your blood supply in times of stress is *excessive* cholesterol. Yet with most fast-food diets this is exactly what happens. The average person in this country takes in about 45 percent of all calories in the form of fats. This is almost *one-third* more than required. (But note that the American Heart Association does not suggest that the answer is to reduce fats to almost *zero*, as many cult nutritionists claim.) (See Chapter 5.)

The occasional meal at your local hamburger chain is harmless. However, if you consistently ate the same meal there three times a day, you could be courting malnutrition as well as obesity and other problems.

8. *The racing heartbeat*

Original benefit

Pumps more blood to the muscles and lungs, to carry more fuel and oxygen to (or from) the battlefront.

Today's drawback

High blood pressure. If unchecked, it could lead to strokes, bursting of an aneurysm, or a host of lesser problems.

This condition could also lead to the "big one"—a fatal heart attack—in anyone over the age of fifteen. If you already have cholesterol deposits in your coronary arteries (and autopsies of young American soldiers have shown that this is alarmingly common), your heart may be barely keeping up with routine demands. Any additional push from excess stress—such as an argument, too much exercise, or heat prostration—could be the last straw.

As seen by the shocking death of Jim Fixx, a leader in the field of jogging, apparent fitness alone does not guarantee immunity.* If you are under excessive stress, or have poor lifestyle habits, or a bad family history, consult your doctor on a regular basis for thorough checks. Even modern tools such as stress EKGs, echocardiograms, and coronary angiograms are not completely foolproof. However, most cases of heart attack would have benefited from earlier testing.

---

*Even Jim Fixx had warnings in his past history, and in his family history, that would have been obvious in a medical investigation and workup. The fact that he apparently was long overdue for a medical checkup should be a warning to us all.

Coronary bypass surgery has become as safe as an ordinary gall bladder removal in terms of risks, and has prevented catastrophe in thousands of patients.

There is a common false security in thinking that your first heart attack will be a small one, and that medical marvels can come to the rescue thereafter. The first warning that your heart is in trouble could well be your last breath.

Ultimately, seeing your doctor isn't going to be enough help unless you are willing to heed his or her advice. You must have the versatility to correct your weak choices, for example, smoking, obesity, wrong job. (See Chapter 3.)

9. Increased air supply

The nostrils flare, the throat dilates, all the air passages in the lungs dilate, and the breathing becomes deeper and more rapid.

Original benefit

Provides the extra supplies of oxygen to feed the increased blood supply coming into the lungs.

Today's drawbacks

Disastrous if you are a smoker or live with one. Even if you do *not* increase the number of cigarettes smoked when under stress (most smokers do), the penetration and damage that each stick of poison gas can wreak is greatly amplified during stress. It makes matters just that much worse when you choose to increase the actual number of cigarettes smoked in response to your stress.

10. The blood (and the plot) thickens

This is due to increased production of red and white blood cells from the marrow. It is also due to the squeezing of the spleen to inject its stored thick paste of blood cells and clotting factors into the bloodstream.

Original benefit

More capacity to carry oxygen, fight infections, and stop bleeding from a wound.

Today's drawback

Strokes, heart attacks, or an embolus can all be encouraged by having the blood turn to sludge under stress. (This is yet another reason why I recommend drinking at least eight glasses of water per day—unless you are an uncontrolled epileptic. It helps dilute your blood.) Blood thinning drugs have long been available, and studies suggest that even less than one adult aspirin per day might help. However, consult your doctor to have yourself and your blood investigated to see what might be needed in your context. As a general principle, I recommend staying away from pills as a long-term response to stress, due to possible unknown side effects.

11. The skin "crawls," pales, and sweats

Original benefit

The skin, the largest organ in the body, has all its hairs stand up on end. This is a vestige left from some of our "fur-fathers." It was useful in increasing the overall appearance of size. The bristling of hairs also heightens our sense of touch. It acts much like a cat's whiskers in the dark, providing a sort of "radar" to detect our closest environment.

The pallor of the skin results from the diverting of its blood to the "war machine" (muscles, heart, and lungs). The effect is to reduce the blood loss from any lacerations.

Under stress, the skin also sweats. This is to provide coolness for the underlying, overheated muscles.

Today's drawback

Social leprosy. The dreaded (at least in TV commercials) traid of clammy hands, pasty face, and stained armpits. Also, sweating decreases the skin's resistance to electricity, which can be easily measured. This will give you away every time in the modern lie detector test (assuming you find telling lies to be stressful).

12. All five senses become acute

Original benefit

This brings the body to its peak of function. It explains why thrill seekers feel they are most alive when doing something very stressful.

Overall mental performance is also improved, with greatly increased concentration, as anyone who ever faced a deadline in school or work knows well.

Eyes—pupils dilate to allow better night vision, and give better peripheral vision when in battle.

Ears—hearing becomes more acute.

Touch—enhanced by the hair response (see response number 11).

Taste, smell—enhanced.

Today's drawback

The major drawback today is the high error rate that occurs after excessive stresses. It seems that the senses "burn out" after unrelenting stress, and become *less* efficient. The person becomes less observant of details around him or her, pays little attention to tastes or smells, tunes out whole conversations, and ignores touch.

For years, comedians have found humor in this state of vulnerability. The very time one is trying to look one's pompous best at a society cocktail party is the time one will inadvertently thrust one's swizzle stick up one's nose.

Knowing when your stresses and this error rate are high could save your life. For example, if you have just had one of your major door-slamming arguments at home, this is the worst time to jump into your car and squeal rubber all the way down the street. Another risky trip is the drive home from the hospital with a brand new baby, even though this stressor is a happy event. When under extreme stress, remember to be careful not to undertake any potentially dangerous activity such as working with power tools or machines, or climbing heights. Stress may also affect the eyes as its only target. I have seen cases in which stress overload first manifests itself with sudden blindness due to detached retinas.

The only other serious drawback to the reaction of the senses is the aggravation of certain eye conditions such as glaucoma by the dilating pupil. An interesting sidelight is that your eyes will certainly betray you when you are under stress. Eyes are our most common "window" to the truth. This is why the bad guys in movies wear sunglasses, and why people who don't look you in the eye during a conversation are perceived to be "shifty" and untrustworthy.

Your eyes can also give away your feelings when presented with pleasant stresses. See Figure 2.1.

Figure 2.1

Pupil size is easily measured, and a good indicator of the different stresses experienced by individuals. When presented with a stresser (in this case a pleasant one), consistent differences between men and women will usually be noted. The first picture will generally dilate the pupils of the women readers.

The second picture will generally dilate the pupils of the men.

The third picture is a control. If this one dilates your pupils you need help!

Stress: cultural and personal factors

Although we have spoken of responses to stress as being fairly general, there can be quite marked differences in response depending on cultural or personal background and differences in gender (see Figure 2.1). The stress of crowded families in North America tends to be equated with high crime and juvenile delinquency, but far greater crowding in Hong Kong and Tokyo does not seem to lead to similar crime levels there. (Could this be because everyone there knows karate and judo?)

On the day that the First World War broke out, there was mass hysteria in front of the Paris Bourse, with people angrily trying to withdraw their money from the stock market. By contrast, on the same day in London, the scene outside the stock exchange was calm. People lined up in single file, quietly reading newspapers as they waited. The ingrained tradition of the British "stiff upper lip" obviously had an effect on how Britons responded. This, of course, is not to say that one response is better than another; we are merely illustrating differences in culture and upbringing.

Figure 2.2

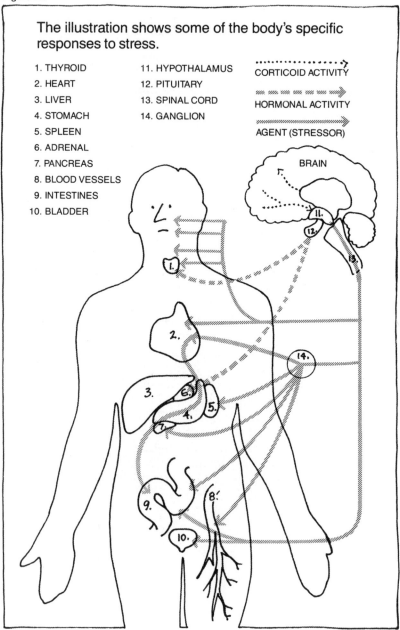

The illustration shows some of the body's specific responses to stress.

1. THYROID
2. HEART
3. LIVER
4. STOMACH
5. SPLEEN
6. ADRENAL
7. PANCREAS
8. BLOOD VESSELS
9. INTESTINES
10. BLADDER
11. HYPOTHALAMUS
12. PITUITARY
13. SPINAL CORD
14. GANGLION

CORTICOID ACTIVITY

HORMONAL ACTIVITY

AGENT (STRESSOR)

BRAIN

Paris Bourse, 1914, the day World War I broke out.

London Stock Exchange, 1914, same day.

Childraising and training for stress

An individual's response to stress can be modi-fied as early as in the cradle and all during one's upbringing. For example, many of the adults I see who do poorly under stress share a common mistake during their formative years—parents who try to "protect" them from all possible stresses. Thus, the "protected" child who has never had to look a waiter in the eye and order his own food during family outings may never learn to look *anyone* in the eye during conversa-tions. (One of my great pet peeves is trying to communicate with a fully grown teenager who shuffles and stares at the ground while mommy or daddy helpfully intercepts all my questions. This adolescent will still be getting wake-up calls in his forties, just in case his alarm clock fails!) This is also one of the reasons many self-made rich and famous personalities have prob-lems with their children. The parent, having gone through considerable poverty on the way to success, wrongfully assumes that this stress was bad for him or her. The attitude of "I may have started out poor but no child (or spouse) of mine is ever going to have to worry about money" deprives the child of ever learning the value of hard work, and undermines the devel-opment of self-esteem and confidence. The child thus spoiled by a well-intentioned paren-tal desire to *save* children from stress will eventually, when forced to meet stresses on his own, be certain to become a *victim*. As I have said before, stress is not an enemy, but your ally, *if* properly managed.

On the other hand, children can be actively raised to *manage* stress, and develop winning responses that will last a lifetime. These are the children that we see to have "leadership" and "self-confident" and independent qualities that help them rise above the crowd in adult years.

It is quite obvious that the stresses of publicity that are placed upon a member of the royal family such as Prince Charles are far greater than most people can be expected to endure. His ability to withstand these pressures can be related directly to his upbringing, since he was trained right from the start in how to handle himself under fire. It would appear that, for this very reason, there is considerable sense in requiring monarchs to marry peers rather than commoners. Princess Diana's upbringing, and the stress of a royal courtship, demonstrated her ability to handle the immense pressures of the spotlight with grace.

Response to stress

People have the ability to choose to respond to stresses in one of two basic ways. They can choose either the *syntoxic* response (the ignoring response), or the *catatoxic* response (fight or flight). A man could well choose the catatoxic response when his wife is being insulted from two rows back in the theater. When he confronts the heckler and learns that the man is six-feet-five-inches and a professional boxer, he may suddenly reverse his field and choose the safer syntoxic response: ignoring the heckler. Again, depending on your upbringing, one or the other of these responses could easily be ingrained to the extent that you do not need to

consciously make a choice. It will be made for
you by your own reflexes.

Human response to any stress, no matter
how trivial, has been well documented by
Dr. Hans Selye. His diagram of the G.A.S., or
General Adaptation Response to Stress, may be
seen in Figure 2.3.

■

Figure 2.3

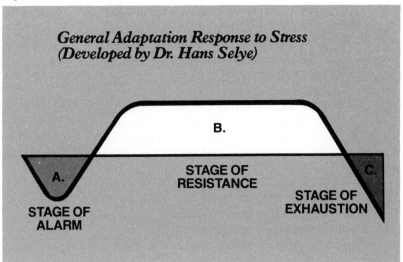

In Stage A, the Alarm Reaction, all of the body's responses to stress come to bear. However, after the stress continues for long enough, the body becomes used to it and enters a Stage of Adaptation, or Resistance. If the stress is unremitting, there is a limit as to how long you can adapt before you enter the Stage of Exhaustion.

Morale studies on Allied bomber crews in the Second World War showed that the Alarm Stage lasted for the first five or six missions over enemy territory. Then the Adaptation Stage set in. But due to the extreme levels of stress, it lasted only about another five missions. After the eleventh flight, morale entered the final Exhaustion Stage. This was marked by a "shell-shocked," war-weary resignation, which was seen to make young men age almost overnight.

The same principles, although far less dramatic, are seen in response to the stresses you face during the day.

That is why it is so important to take a break in the action and incur different stresses (notice I didn't say *less* stress necessarily). Alternate stresses (see Chapter 4) are better than just plowing on with the same ones, as workaholics are prone to do. The true workaholic's level of efficiency will decrease with his or her constant stress levels, to the point where the person will *need* sixteen hours to accomplish what he or she should be able to do in eight.

Selye's G.A.S. model also serves to illustrate the basic stages of your life. Childhood is the first Stage. The Stage of Adaptation or Resistance corresponds to your adult years of health, leading to eventual decline and the Exhaustion Stage at death. The trick is how to lengthen the Stage of Adaptation or Resistance!

3.
The Hanson Scale of Stress Resistance:

It's your choice

Now that we have seen what stress can do, both *to* and *for* your body, you need to know how *much* stress you are facing. It is therefore useful to have measurable "warning lights" for stress overload, to alert you to dangers before something breaks.

Because many stresses have an emotional component, it is difficult to assign an absolute value to them. (For example, the sight of a mouse may be so stressful to some people that they will faint; the same stressor might not even rate a yawn in others.)

The now familiar Holmes-Rahe Scale (see Figure 3.1), published in 1967 attempted to provide some guidelines for stress measurement. It is still valuable today as a benchmark. Holmes and Rahe rated the death of a spouse as 100 units, and marriage as 50 units. Note that 10 of the top 15 stresses on the scale have nothing to do with work. This is a surprise to most people. They expect stress at work, and may be on their guard to defend against it. However, they usually assume that home life is harmless, thus undervaluing the stresses on the spouse who stays at home, or undervaluing their spare time if they both work. As we shall see later, it is only by being aware of your stresses that you can cope with them. You cannot fight an unseen enemy.

Figure 3.1

Holmes-Rahe scale of stress ratings

Use the blanks at the bottom to list any of your stresses that do not appear on the Holmes-Rahe Scale. You can assign numerical rating to your particular stresses by comparing them with those on the scale.

Please note that the ratings apply only to stresses that you have undergone within the past twenty-four months.

Once you have rated all stresses that apply to you, add the numbers to arrive at your total.

LIFE EVENT	VALUE	YOUR SCORE
Death of spouse	100	
Divorce	73	
Marital separation	65	
Jail term	63	
Death of a close family member	63	
Personal injury or illness	53	
Marriage	50	
Fired at work	47	
Marital reconciliation	45	
Retirement	45	
Change in health of family member	44	
Pregnancy	40	
Sex difficulties	39	
Gain of new family member	39	

(continued next page)

Business adjustment	39	
Change in financial state	38	
Death of a close friend	37	
Change to different line of work	36	
Change in number of arguments with spouse	35	
Mortgage over one year's net salary	31	
Foreclosure of mortgage or loan	30	
Change in responsibilities at work	29	
Son or daughter leaving home	29	
Trouble with in-laws	29	
Outstanding personal achievement	28	
Spouse begins or stops work	26	
Begin or end school	26	
Change in living conditions	25	
Revision of personal habits	24	
Trouble with boss	23	
Change in work hours or conditions	20	
Change in residence	20	

Change in schools	20	
Change in recreation	19	
Change in church activities	19	
Change in social activities	18	
Mortgage or loan less than one year's net salary	17	
Change in sleeping habits	16	
Change in number of family get-togethers	15	
Change in eating habits	15	
Vacation	13	
Christmas	12	
Minor violations of the law	11	
Misc:		
Enter your total here.		

If your total is over 300, then you have an *80 percent chance of a serious change in your health within the next year.*

You now have some objective idea of the amount of stress that faces you. If your total score is less than 150 units, you have a 30 percent chance of a serious change in your health within the next year. Up to 300 units gives you a 50 percent chance. More than 300 units gives you an 80 percent chance.

The exact nature of this change in health is highly individual, and will probably involve your weakest link, no matter how healthy you think you are. For example, some people are prone to ulcers, others to heart attacks or sudden alarming irregularities of heartbeat, mental breakdowns, colitis, asthma, or (by virtue of decreased immune responses), infections, and even cancers. By having regular checkups from your doctor, at least *annually* if you have a high stress score, you will gain insight into your own target areas and be better able to prevent crises.

Taking a second look at these statistics through the other end of the binoculars, you may be struck by the fact that 20 percent of people in the high-stress group will have no change in health at all. What makes these people so "bullet-proof"? To discover the answer, it was necessary to devise an additional scale—the Hanson Scale of Stress Resistance. This scale measures your choices in response to stress, and shows you where you can improve.

The Hanson Scale of Stress Resistance shows you 10 choices to weaken yourself, and 10 to strengthen yourself against stress. Once you realize that your life is on the line, and that these choices do not just deal with unimportant habits, it becomes easier to manage your life better and thus tolerate higher levels of stress.

Now let's look at the significance of each of the 10 weak choices on the Hanson Scale.

Figure 3.2

Hanson Scale of Stress Resistance

WEAK CHOICES	SCORE	STRONG CHOICES	SCORE
1. Bad genetics	–10	1. Good genetics	10
2. Insomnia	–20	2. Sense of humor	20
3. Bad diet	–30	3. Right diet	30
4. Obesity	–40	4. Alternate stresses	40
5. Unrealistic goals	–50	5. Realistic goals	50
6. Poisons (including		6. Understanding of	
caffeine)	–60	stress	60
7. Smoking	–70	7. Relaxation skills and	
8. Wrong job	–80	efficient sleep	70
9. Financial distress	–90	8. Thorough job	
10. Unstable home	–100	preparation	80
		9 Financial security	90
		10. Stable home	100
	–550	Resistance Score	+550

Using the Hanson Scale:

You can use the Hanson Scale to determine your stress resistance, which can then be added to your current stresses (Holmes-Rahe score).

Although there will be different *degrees* of each category, assume for the initial purposes of this exercise that any degree gets the full number of points.* (For example, whether you smoke forty cigarettes per day or ten, you still get –70 on your score sheet.) Once you have your basic picture, you can adjust the fine focus by changing these numbers a few points up or down.

---

*These numbers are somewhat arbitrarily assigned, and serve to provide you with a rough guideline only.

We have seen that we share many common animal responses to stress. Of course, as humans, we have only one key advantage over the baboon: *intelligence*. We can use it to make ourselves much stronger than the so-called "dumb" animal. However, as we can see from Figure 3.2, most people's choices in response to stress leave them *weaker* than the animal. Whether such choices are active or unwitting matters not—the results are reduced enjoyment, impaired health, length of life, and, not coincidentally, reduced efficiency and profits in the workplace. However, by choosing your responses intelligently, you can conquer stress, live *better*, and live longer.

The popular "herd instinct" of wrong choices isn't due just to lack of opportunity. As a dramatic example, let me mention a personal experience. I recently toured a modern air traffic control headquarters, where the latest of stress reducers were at hand, for example, a library, sports and hobby facilities, and even the odd rude movie. The controllers are under intense stress, and are usually allowed to work only half of their eight-hour shift, the other half being set aside for relief of tension. At the time I visited, the thoughtfully provided outlets were being completely neglected. People on breaks congregated in the coffee room for gossip and chain-smoked cigarettes. If you are like most people, your exercise bike and fitness-club membership card are both gathering dust. Fitness depends on *motivation,* not tools and toys.

Weak Choice Number 1

Bad Genetics—Minus 10 Points

Although the quality of health and the lifespan of your ancestors is not within your control, it has been said that the key to a long life is to choose your parents carefully. This may not be as important as once thought. Thus a history of relatively early deaths in your family has been given the lowest rating on the Hanson Scale of Stress Resistance. Although this may seem odd, it is generally true that most people's ancestors died prematurely because of what could now be seen as mismanagement (not necessarily of their own doing) of their stresses. In many cases, lives were shortened because of the direct trauma of war, famine, or diseases, which, even if survived, took a very high toll of adaptation "coins." This—along with mismanagement in other areas such as lifestyle, financial, environmental, and retirement planning—may well have contributed to their early demise.

Until very recently, it was virtually unheard of for the majority of the population to do regular and proper exercise for any appreciable part of their lifetimes. Although people on farms tended to derive the benefits of exercise from their everyday work, such people historically also suffered from periods of food shortage due to drought, insects, and so on. Medical care was primitive. With the advances in modern living, most of the causes of your ancestors' deaths would now be treatable. Also, our knowledge of public health has improved. Thus if your family died young of lung cancer, but worked in an asbestos town, this need not be reflected in your own health, assuming you are not being exposed to the same risks.

BAD GENETICS.
If your parents or grandparents died before 65, your score = -10.
Enter your score here.

Of course, if all the males in your family died in their thirties from the same heart disease, and you do not bother seeing a doctor yourself until you are twenty-nine, it is quite likely that you could inherit their "bad luck." The low rating accorded to the genetic factor is not intended to demean the very real risks to those with inherited diseases, but rather to emphasize the numerical rarity of such cases.

Weak Choice Number 2

Insomnia—Minus 20 Points

Although this may not seem like a choice, the fact that sleep can be gained without drugs makes it so. If you are chronically unable to sleep efficiently and awake refreshed, you will not be in very good shape to withstand the following day's stresses. One of the most common reasons for the problem is a racing of the mind through the day's unresolved stresses. We will discuss ways to correct this later.

We must take into consideration how much sleep you as an individual need in the first place. I receive many requests for sleeping pills from elderly patients because they are sleeping only four or five hours per night. Actually, it is quite normal for people to require less sleep as they grow older, and yet the ingrained habit of thinking one requires eight hours is still present. I tell these patients that the only way they could be given the additional three hours of sleep a night would be through a general anesthetic. They do not, in fact, have true insomnia.

Stimulants such as caffeine and alcohol will interfere with a good sleep, as will Type A behavior (see Chapter 8), a large meal before bedtime, a snoring spouse, or a crying baby. However, for those who wake up each morning feeling fatigued, as if they need another eight hours to perform efficiently, there are many relaxation techniques that are quite valuable. (See Chapter 4.)

INSOMNIA.
Your score if you
have chosen it = –20.
Enter your score here.

Weak Choice Number 3

Bad Diet—Minus 30 Points

If you eat too many or too few calories, the wrong foods, or if you eat too quickly, you are *choosing* to greatly weaken your resistance to stress. Fad diets tend to leave out at least one of the six key food elements (carbohydrates, fats, protein, fiber, water, or vitamins), and thus should be avoided. Excess salt (usually in the form of snack foods with the salt already added) can be harmful to your blood pressure, and increase fluid loads on the heart and kidneys. Insufficient fluid intake (less than eight glasses of water per day) is detrimental to the viscosity of the blood and the function of the kidneys.

BAD DIET. Your score if you choose to have one = –30. Enter your score here.

Self-medication with megadoses of minerals and vitamins can also be very hazardous. I will discuss nutrition and diet in detail later in this book. If you are not sure if you have a bad diet, enter your score after you have read Chapter 5.

Weak Choice Number 4

Obesity—Minus 40 Points

This is a weighty subject. (See Chapter 6.) The body has a tendency to *lose* weight without changing diet when under stress. So it actually requires determined overeating to stay fat.

But let's take a closer look at obesity, and try to understand it better. Obesity is not a problem: it's only the *result* of a problem. Usually the root problem is one of these:

1. Boredom.
2. Excess stress.
3. Lifestyle and peer pressure.
4. Poor self-image.
5. All of the above.

People who choose to eat in response to stress freely admit that they don't do it out of hunger. In fact, how could they? Their stomachs are rarely empty. This situation is quite pitiable.

Obesity requires cooperation and careful work with your doctor, in order to find solutions for the real underlying problems. Surgical cures, which include everything from wiring the teeth shut to bypassing part of the stomach and loops of intestines, are not usually the long-term answers (short of constructing a single tube to join the mouth to the rectum). Often childhood habits such as being forced to finish everything on your plate, and being rewarded with food instead of hugs when you did something right, have led to overeating. But as adults we can, with help, overcome the effects of such childhood conditioning.

Even being 10 percent over your *ideal weight* (not from insurance charts, but the weight at which you look and feel the best in your bathing suit) is a detriment to your health and well-being. Jockeys know that as little as a ten-pound weight gain can decrease the performance of the horse under the rider; just imagine the effect of even ten extra pounds on your own legs.

Morbid obesity can be defined as being more than double your ideal weight. The statistics relating to it are truly frightening. When I see patients in their twenties with this sort of excess weight, I can tell them that they will statistically have a great deal of difficulty surviving to the age of fifty unless they change their ways.

In spite of all the diet articles we are faced with in so many magazines and books, I find most people still don't choose to eat properly. Animals in the wild would not survive if they were as much overweight as many humans are. (Besides humans, the only other pathologically obese creatures are domestic pets fed by humans.)

OBESITY.
Your score if you choose to be fat = −40.
Enter your score here.

The effects of obesity are more than aesthetics, or the trembling of the knees under the massive weight of the body. The heart will not last as many years; other areas of the body that are harmed by obesity include the lungs, the liver, and the pancreas (diabetes may result). This subject is dealt with more fully in Chapter 6; also see the "eat *normally*" way to lose weight in Chapter 7.

Weak Choice Number 5

Unrealistic Goals—Minus 50 Points

The short person who dreams of being a basketball player, and the tall person who wants to be a jockey . . . both are being unrealistic. Unless they change their goals, they will be doomed to failure, as measured by their own ambitions. The continual unhappiness resulting from unrealistic goals can have a very negative effect on a person's ability to resist stress. Through the magic of television, most people now leave school with high expectations regarding their future lifestyles. Yet they may be ill-prepared to put in the hours of work and training necessary to achieve the rewards they expect. This can lead to tremendous dissatisfaction, and is responsible for some of the frustration found among the unemployed in the under-twenty-five age group today.

However, our society does seem to be changing. Up until recently, most parents encouraged their children to pursue a white-collar education or training. In the last few years, the realities of a crowded job market have dictated that a university degree is no longer the guarantee of success. Students now flock to courses or apprenticeships that teach them a salable skill, suited to their aptitudes and interests. In this way we are able to produce more skilled workers at all levels. A university education in its purest sense is unfettered exercise for the mind, and as such is very useful for *some* students, but certainly not *all*. Having studied *Don Quixote* for three years may not necessarily impress the personnel manager on your next job hunt.

UNREALISTIC GOALS. Your score if you choose to have them = –50. Enter your score here.

Realistic, as opposed to unrealistic, goals will be discussed in Chapter 4.

Weak Choice Number 6

Poisons—Minus 60 Points

I use the rather strong word *poisons* to cover the broad category of toxins, drugs, and excessive caffeine taken in response to stress. The most common one is alcohol.

Alcohol

Alcohol in moderation (one to two ounces per day, or one to two glasses of wine or beer) can be harmless enough except during pregnancy. In fact, some evidence now suggests that your cholesterol level can in fact be reduced by this sort of moderate intake. However, drinks in excess of this amount quickly cross over into the toxic side. Excessive alcohol interferes with sleep patterns and the integrity of the stomach lining, It can cause cirrhosis of the liver, headaches, and a host of other problems. It can lead to atrophy of the testicles in males and of the ovaries in females, to the point where libido is nonexistent. Most importantly, excessive alcohol consumption can destroy irreplaceable brain cells.

Alcohol at bedtime—with its paradoxical delayed stimulative action—interferes with efficient sleep. Alcohol in excess also causes unbelievable *premature aging.* If you could see the birth certificate of the typical street "wino," who looks about ninety years old, you would be truly shocked. He might be only in his thirties; at autopsy every internal organ would show advanced aging. Whenever I see someone who is much older in appearance than in stated years, alcoholism is the first condition that I suspect.

Tranquilizers

Another major type of poison is the tranquilizer family of drugs. The most important source of these drugs, unfortunately, can be the medical profession itself. Tranquilizers such as Valium are the most widely used prescription drugs today. The degree of public dependence on tranquilizers to relieve stress is appalling. Help for stress does not come in pill form. Your treatments should aim at the *cause* of the stress, not the end *result*. (The other two drugs in the top three are Tagamet for stomach ulcers, and Inderol for blood pressure, angina, and migraines—conditions directly related to stress.)

Each typical small-sized tranquilizer, which is normally taken several times per day, requires more than twenty-four hours to be fully cleared from the body. Thus they are never out of the bloodstream, if taken daily, even just at bedtime for insomnia. All that long-term tranquilizers will do is become habit-forming, and decrease your mental alertness, making it more difficult for you to organize or solve your problems.

Tranquilizers do have an occasional short-term role in the management of acute crises. The legitimate and useful role of longer term tranquilizers in the treatment of true psychiatric pathology is another subject, and is beyond the scope of this book.

Caffeine

Reaching for that nice hot cup of coffee or tea when under stress has become one of life's more popular pleasures. Certainly one cup of coffee or two cups of tea per day will not cause any real harm. However, as with alcohol, more than this can become detrimental if *caffeine* is present.

Some of the main sources of caffeine are:

mg of Caffeine

Coffee
  Instant—one cup *104*
  Percolated—one cup. *192*
  Strong Drip—one cup. *240*
Tea—one cup *48-72*
Colas—one glass *27-54*
Chocolate, Hot, one small cup *15*

If you are used to drinking an instant coffee, then a decaffeinated instant would be suggested as a substitute. If you usually grind your own beans at home before each potful, then the decaffeinated instants (like the regular instants) would naturally suffer by comparison. Freshly ground decaffeinated whole beans would make a virtually indistinguishable substitute here because caffeine itself is an odorless and tasteless ingredient.

Of course, coffee and tea have other chemicals besides caffeine. I do not necessarily endorse these—much is yet unknown about them. In the strictly analytical sense, the best that can be said for coffee and tea is that they are a nutritional zero, and just expensive hot brown water.

However, due to their immense followings, it would not be realistic to assume their use will ever be discontinued. Thus, you should try to find a suitable decaffeinated coffee or tea (such as an herbal tea) that satisfies your tastes and fulfills your desire for a hot drink that is relaxing. (The reason it seems more relaxing is that your conversation partner cannot just gulp it down and walk off.) Since coffee or tea and cigarettes are a two-handed habit in most smokers, switching to ice water may have the added benefit of reducing the automatic urge to light up during "coffee" breaks.

What does caffeine do to harm you? Plenty. As little as two and a half cups per day (400 mg) can double the adrenalin in your bloodstream, at a time when your body is already trying to do the same thing in response to stress. Caffeine can result in inefficient sleep when taken in the late evening. Although falling asleep may be easy, your sleep is inefficient, and you can't fully wake up the next morning until you have your cup of coffee, and so the cycle goes on.

Quite apart from the controversial possibilities of caffeine causing cancer (which I won't even bother discussing here, as they are still being debated), excess caffeine is known to fiercely aggravate stomach ulcers. When you are under stress, your stomach normally shuts down, as we have seen. Any food and drink that is put into it at that time tends to sit there longer than it would normally. Thus the caffeine has a chance to do even more damage to your stomach lining. At the other end of the line, caffeine can also magnify the problems of colitis. Even hemorrhoids are known to be made worse in many people by the oral consumption of caffeine. The increased energy that is artificially gained from caffeine also puts increased demands on your heart. This may tip the scales toward angina in an already compromised heart that is working to capacity.

As if all this weren't enough, caffeine (even just two cups of coffee per day) can cause breast lumps in many women. I have found caffeine to be a frequent factor in breast problems. The cessation of caffeine consumption will help many women who suffer from tender breasts at or before the time of their periods, or from generally cystic and "ropy" breasts. Caffeine *does not* cause breast cancer as such. However, by encouraging harmless cysts, it certainly makes the detection of new lumps more difficult.

POISONS.
Your score if you
choose to abuse = *-60.*
Enter your score here.

Surprisingly, excess caffeine consumption rates as the *easiest* of all habits to give up, according to my patients.

Weak Choice Number 7

Smoking—Minus 70 Points

This is a common and disastrous response to stress, and is the number one preventable health hazard in the world. The very idea of rolling up a leaf, sticking it in your face, and setting fire to it does seem to defy intelligent explanation. Besides, think about what it does to your body.

I have often seen pregnant mothers with conscientious concerns about what foods will be best for the unborn baby and whether the water should be boiled before drinking. Often such mothers stoically refuse to take even the safest medication to relieve a migraine. These concerns are welcome, and in most cases fully justified.

Yet it is a source of amazement to me that some of these same mothers-to-be will blithely inhale a pack of cigarettes per day, ignoring the incredible, constant, and devastating damage to the developing fetus. Smoking during pregnancy is nothing other than a prenatal form of child abuse. Many obstetricians today are even refusing to accept responsibility for prenatal patients who continue to smoke during pregnancy.

The effects of this child abuse-in-utero, of course, persist into childhood if either parent smokes in the house. Evidence now suggests that second-hand smoke can stunt both physical and mental development, and cause a much higher incidence of children's visits to the doctor for bronchitis, headache, asthma, head

colds, and allergy-related conditions. It is a
further source of amazement to me to see intelligent and loving parents refuse to quit smoking
cigarettes in spite of persisting hardships to
their children, proven by the allergist or asthma
specialist to be directly related to smoking.

Even more significant than their role
as an agent of *child* abuse, cigarettes are an
unparalleled form of *self*-abuse. During stress,
when lungs are already being dilated and sucking in air to the maximum capacity, the inhaled
cigarette smoke is able to do its maximum
amount of damage. The fact that all the blood
vessels in the body, including the coronary
arteries, are known to clamp down severely
when even one cigarette is inhaled makes it easy
to see why smoking can push you closer toward
heart attack pains.

Probably we have all seen vivid pictures or
films about the effects of cigarettes on the circulation of blood to the heart, stomach, skin,
and other organs. Literature abounds on the
subject of the ill effects of cigarette smoking, to
the extent that public financing of even more
studies on smoking are wasteful of medical
research dollars. We all know by this time that
cigarette smoke is a proven killer. However,
cigarette sales have remained relatively stable.
They tend to decline only when taxes become
too high for the market to pay.

It is interesting to note that when teenage
girls are left out of the calculations, statistics
show the majority of North American adults do
not smoke. This is certainly a sign of discre-
tion, and an improvement over the past. It is

also a clear indication that smokers are killing themselves off faster than new recruits can be found.

Smoking badly damages virtually every organ in the body. It is responsible for thousands of deaths from heart attacks and stomach ulcers. Approximately 30 percent of all cancers are related to smoking. This includes lung cancer, throat cancer, and cancer of the bladder, to name but a few. Even second-hand smoke can be very dangerous, particularly to patients with angina. Such patients often get chest pains simply by walking into a smoky room. "Careless" smoking is also a major cause of deaths, severe burns, and property loss.

Remember, if you are a smoker, you may think your lungs are in great shape. You may be falsely lulled by the memory of an aged family member who smoked. But until you try to do extensive exercise (like running a few miles or skiing at high altitudes) or have your pulmonary functions measured by your doctor, you will probably have no idea how bad your lungs are. You may not notice your lung deterioration until you can no longer climb stairs without having to pause for a breath, and no longer finish a sentence without sucking for air. These are predictable and irreversible manifestations of late stage emphysema, and have nothing to do with the state of your muscles.

SMOKING.
Your choice of you choose to do it = −70.
Enter your score here.

The only way to salvage the remaining lung tissue at this stage is to quit your cigarettes. There is no dietary supplement, series of exercises, vitamin, or magic potion that will negate the poisonous effects of inhaled tobacco smoke.

Weak Choice Number 8

Wrong Job—Minus 80 Points

Are you happy in your work? If not, you are committing one of the worst "offenses" against yourself. Even if you have realistic goals in terms of your ultimate financial and other achievements, you may have chosen the wrong job for your own personality and aptitudes. This wrong choice can be one of the biggest handicaps of all. Lack of satisfaction on the job breeds discontent, lowered self-image, brooding, moody behavior, and often increased arguments at home with the family. This can be just as true if you are "over-educated for the job," as if you are undereducated and poorly prepared.

It may seem unlikely that anybody would willingly choose the wrong job for himself or herself. But in fact it does often occur, for various reasons. For example, Dr. Laurence Peter, author of *The Peter Principle*, has demonstrated that it is all too common for people in a job hierarchy to continue to be promoted until they reach their level of incompetence.

The corollary of this is that, in any hierarchy, each person tends to rise until he or she becomes incompetent at a job. It is at that level that he or she stays, being considered unsuitable for further promotion. (If this is commonly true, the majority of jobs are held by incompetents.) This situation would reduce the stress resistance of the corporation as a whole, and would certainly impair the individual's ability to resist stress.

Keep in mind, you need not be a passive bystander; you can say "no" to a promotion above your area of competence. You can ask for your old job back if you recognize unhappiness resulting from your last promotion. Or you could even quit and find more suitable work elsewhere.

Inadequate education often prevents people from doing work they enjoy. But it is possible to go into retraining programs. You can still be the architect of your own destiny to a large extent.

WRONG JOB.
Your score if you have one = –80.
Enter your score here.

Never underestimate the importance of *knowing yourself,* in order to assess the types of work that are best suited to your strengths and weaknesses. See the appendix to find out which social style quadrant you are in, and to help you find job categories that would be appropriate.

Weak Choice Number 9

Financial Distress—Minus 90 Points

As evidenced in the stock market crash of 1929, a financial crisis can evoke a lot of ledge-jumping. The detrimental effects of having the financial "alligators" snapping at your heels are seen both in the acute fall from wealth and the chronic oppression of poverty. Financial distress may also apply to those between the two extremes—people who are working hard and making a good wage, but lack perspective, discipline, and organization in managing their money. The difference between spending 5 percent *more* than you earn and spending 5 percent *less* than you earn separates financial distress from comfort.

The cash lost through the inefficiencies of mismanagement could often be enough to finance stress reduction measures such as vacations, treats, or part-time help around the home. Without stress reduction, the tendency is for you to continue to spin your wheels, ultimately undermine both your health and your ability to perform well in your job, thus continuing to earn.

When I see a patient with chest or stomach pains, a headache, or even depression, I always include in my assessment questions about how things are going financially. Very often the rest of the medical history will be negative, but it is the fiscal problems that are causing the trouble. In a case like this, a good financial adviser can often help more than a doctor.

FINANCIAL DISTRESS. Your score if you have it = –90. Enter your score here.

71

Weak Choice Number 10

Unstable Home and Social Support— Minus 100 Points

This rates the highest score on our list of conditions that reduce your resistance to stress. Yet the typical workaholic, when under stress, tends to de-emphasize his or her family and friends as being inconsequential. In fact, nothing could be further from the truth. Such an attitude is definitely likely to end in marital strife or even breakup, which will further add to the stress score. It may also bring with it a

host of other stresses as listed by Holmes and Rahe; for example, change in the number of arguments with the spouse, having a son or daughter leave home, trouble with in-laws, change in living conditions, revision of personal habits, trouble with boss, change in work hours or conditions, change in residence, change in social activities and sexual problems.

By choosing to relegate family and friends to the back seat in your life, you could be gravely weakening your stress resistance, as well as shortening your life. It is extremely important that due emphasis be placed on the safety net of family, friends—and even pets if you wish. They provide much-needed support. If this simple fact is ignored, you may be unlikely to live long enough to reap the rewards of all that hard work and eventually even the quality of your work itself will suffer through "burnout." There are a few people in this world who deliberately choose to be "loners," but they do not tend to be among the long livers.

Reach out and touch those around you. As well as providing reassurance, and aiding communications, it can help you live longer. Frequently touching (nonsexual) is common in most societies, but we still retain a certain constipated resistance to it in North America.

UNSTABLE HOME AND SOCIAL SUPPORT.
Your score if you choose this = –100. Enter your score here.

How did you do?

WEAK CHOICES	POSSIBLE SCORE	ENTER YOUR SCORE
1. Bad genetics	10	
2. Insomnia	–20	
3. Bad Diet	–30	
4. Obesity	–40	
5. Unrealistic goals	–50	
6. Poisons (including caffeine)	–60	
7. Smoking	–70	
8. Wrong job	–80	
9. Financial distress	–90	
10. Unstable home	–100	
Total score if you made all the wrong choices = –550	**YOUR TOTAL**	

All right, now you have a minus score total. To put this in perspective, keep in mind that the best score is *zero*. Anything over –10 should be improved. Now you're ready to start calculating your positive responses to stress—to work out your plus score on the "strong" side of the Hanson Scale. Read on. . . .

The benefits of touching

In a recent experiment, a young schoolgirl was asked to give a poetry reading to a group of peers in her home. Blood pressure and pulse monitors were connected to a graph. Predictably, with the "stage fright" of performing, both of these parameters quickly rose and stayed high throughout her reading. However, when the girl's cat jumped up on her lap for a cuddle, she absent-mindedly began petting it as she continued reading. Both her blood pressure and her pulse rate plummeted back to normal. Similar experiments with adults and the elderly confirm the universality of this effect. Pets do help counteract the effects of stress.

4.
The
Hanson Scale:

Ten choices to be strong

Now that we have considered 10 weak choices in response to stress, let's look at 10 positive choices.

These 10 responses will give you the basis for defense against stress, in much the same way as the learned skills of judo assist in neutralizing the energy of an onrushing attacker.

By and large, the steps we are about to discuss require a conscious choice on your part, if you have not been in the habit of following them. However, they can soon become just as much a part of your conditioned reflexes as some of the bad (and often unconscious) choices, such as reaching for a cigarette. Most of the responses I am about to recommend are enjoyable; none require monastic self-denial.

The end result will be to add more years to your life, and more life to your years. If you master these, you will be able to thrive under pressure, and learn the true Joy of Stress.

Strong Choice Number 1

Good Genetics—Plus 10 Points

*GOOD GENETICS.
If your ancestors lived to
a ripe old age,
your score = +10.
Enter your score here.*

Although this is the only item on the scale that you can't choose, I include it for its undeniable relevance. Just as we have seen that bad genetics need not spell out an automatic shortening of lifespan, a good genetic history by itself should not give false confidence. For example, if all your ancestors on the farm lived to be over ninety, and you have now moved into the city and face the totally different stresses of fighting the modern time clock, there is no guarantee that you will share their good fortune. However, if you were to copy the good points of their lifestyle and make the correct choices in response to your new stresses, then their history of longevity could certainly help you.

In any event, rather than dwelling on ancestors, it is better to plan for a lasting close relationship with your descendants. You should aim to live at least long enough to allow your children to come home and show you their old-age security cards!

Strong Choice Number 2

Sense of Humor—Plus 20 Points

Research suggests that laughter increases the body's level of endorphins. This can in fact "ease the pain" and help improve resistance to disease.

Norman Cousins became famous for his ability to laugh in the face of a dire medical prognosis. He collected all the humorous material he could in the form of books, movies, and so on, and then literally laughed himself back into health. Humor certainly ignites the will to live, which if missing, makes the recovery process much more difficult. One of the reasons why an entertaining night of comedy leaves the audience feeling so good is that it helps them forget their woes, and in fact even obtain some true medical benefit in defending themselves against their stresses.

So it seems we should not begrudge the high salaries of entertainers. Part of the value of laughter is that it enables you to gain new perspectives on your problems. It often makes you realize that others have the same problems, and that you are not alone. A popular style of humor is to use the technique of making the listener feel superior . . . to the comedian, or to mothers-in-law, or to minority groups. However, the benefit of humor cannot be maximized until you can laugh at *yourself.* (If you cannot laugh at yourself, you will find plenty of volunteers to do it for you!)

SENSE OF HUMOR.
Your score if you've got one = +20.
Enter your score here.

Strong Choice Number 3

The Right Diet—Plus 30 Points

The best diet for stress is one that is:

1. Natural (with as few additives as possible).

2. Providing the right number of *calories* to maintain your ideal body weight.

3. Eaten at a reasonable pace.

4. Balanced (see Chapter 5).

   • 50 percent carbohydrates, with less than 10 percent of this being simple sugars, and the rest being complex carbohydrates such as pasta, rice, whole grain breads, and cereals.

   • 30-35 percent fats, including both polyunsaturated fats and saturated fats; for example, salad oils, eggs, butter, margarine, and cheese.

   • 15-20 percent protein (depending on age); for example, dairy products, meats, vegetables.

     Traditionally, it was thought that a high protein meal was the best for periods of stress. This is why the pregame meal for most boxers was a large steak. However, experiments have shown that relegating protein to the smallest portion on your plate in fact can more than double your effective energy output and endurance as compared to a meal of pure protein.

   • 50 grams of fiber; for example, beans, bran cereals, high-fiber biscuits, breads.

- Sufficient vitamins and minerals—either from your natural foods or, more realistically, with a little help from a single vitamin supplement each day. (See Appendix.)

- Eight glasses of water per day. If you don't like your local tap water, then try bottled water. (See page 134.)

In connection with balanced diet, let's take the example of an average person about to begin a stressful day at work. Rather than choosing a heavy breakfast of high fat and sugar content, this person should choose a *balanced* breakfast. About 50 percent should be carbohydrate (for example, in high fiber toast and cereal). The remainder should be divided between protein and fats (such as milk and eggs).

Prior to the stress of endurance events such as marathon running, it is a common practice to increase glycogen stores of energy in the muscles by carbohydrate loading for a few days, but in practical terms the balanced approach is better for normal stresses.

The same principles apply to any meal. In particular, the "free" expense account lunch presents the wrong temptations. Typically high in calories and often alcohol, and low enough in fiber and carbohydrates to be unbalanced, the meal can sit heavily in the stomach.

The unwitting executive may arrive back at the office all geared up for a snooze instead of action. If the lunch was conducted under the stressful constraints of a busy working day, the stomach, as we have seen, has largely shut down. It would be better to have more calories at breakfast and dinner in that case, and skip a big meal at lunch.

RIGHT DIET.
Your score if you
have it = +30.
Enter your score here.

Your total calories can be divided in any way you like during the day, including snacks. However I recommend not eating any large meals within three hours of bedtime since this can lead to sleep disturbance and gastrointestinal upset.

EAT SLOWLY: Remember a meal is not a race.

On a stressful day, as we have seen, your stomach is likely to be shut down. Thus poorly chewed food, and drinks consumed in a hurry, will tend to sit like a tin lunch bucket under your rib cage for several hours.

We all know that good manners dictate a slow rate of eating, but most of us find the admonishments to chew your food at least ten times to be a little pediatric. What is clearly needed is a new list of *adult* tips for slower eating. Based on thousands of patient interviews, I have distilled the following hints:

- Sit down.
- Try chewing your food before swallowing it.
- Wait until the waiter has finished placing your meal in front of you before you start eating.
- Relax your death grip on your cutlery—no one is going to take it away.
- Cut your food into more than two pieces.
- Remember to take the aluminum foil off your potato before eating it.
- Leave time for breathing between mouthfuls.
- Try an argument, or talk about yourself: whoever does the most talking usually finishes eating last.
- Never try eating to break dance music.
- Be obsequious—try to think of fatuous compliments for your hostess between mouthfuls.

Strong Choice Number 4

Alternate Stresses—Plus 40 Points

If you're under a great deal of daily stress, it is not good enough to lie down and stare at the ceiling or rattle around the TV dial all evening. Your mind continues to rehash the day's problems and thus perpetuates your stress. In 1960, a researcher in experiments on sensory deprivation, showed that, even when paid $20 per day, student volunteers could not stay in bed for more than two or three days without any activity. Going from *too much* stress to *too little* stress is obviously like jumping out of the frying pan into the fire.

The best way to unwind, it has been found, is to switch to something else that is also stressful. This alternate stress should be something that requires full concentration, but that involves *different* circuits of the brain and body. Thus, such obviously stressful activities as roller coaster rides, mountain climbing, white water boating, parachuting, racquet sports, and surfing can all have a tremendous value in the reduction of your ordinary stresses. An activity of this nature forces you to completely forget about your routine stresses. The alternate stresses for your *mind* could well be sedentary, such as music, reading, or crafts, but make sure you still leave at least three hours per week for the alternate stresses for your *body*. (This is why championship chess players now have a vigorous exercise routine in their training.)

The important point is that what you choose to do should be an *alternate* exercise. A professional baseball pitcher, on a day off, would not be reducing stress by playing more baseball. The main benefit comes from using *different* circuits. The tennis pro, for example, may get some relief from stress by tackling a desk job such as financial management or playing the stock markets. On the other hand, the professional financial expert would benefit more from playing competitive tennis as a break in his or her routine.

Another aspect of this in connection with longevity is that, without an interest in some alternate activities, you may well have little else of interest in your life when you reach retirement age. As we have seen in the introduction, this lack of stress can be fatal. Furthermore, senility can set in at any age with the absence of stimulation. Being dull and boring is certainly not restricted to the elderly, as anyone who has ever attended a cocktail party can attest to.

Exercise in itself is extremely important. If your job does not give you the degree of exercise that the ski pro or (pre-chain-saw era) lumberjack would obtain, then your alternative stresses should certainly provide it. Your body is a finely tuned instrument, but the muscles will not retain their tone, shape, or function if you are slack about exercising them. It has been shown that cardiac function in seventy-year-olds who have been keeping fit all their lives is actually better than that in untrained twenty-year-olds. If you leave fitness until your retirement years, you can still improve upon the odds of survival and give your heart the function of an untrained forty-year-old, but obviously it would be better to stay in shape all along.

The problem of fitness does not relate merely to adults. North Americans tend to start degenerating as early as age six, when they

begin "organized" school activities. They usually have no regular exercise ritual at school, and develop a tendency toward sedentary leisure activities such as watching television and playing computer games. It behooves us to remember that fitness is an acquired lifestyle habit, and should start in childhood. If you have been out of shape throughout all of your adult life, you should not embark upon any exercise program without having a thorough examination by your doctor. More to the point, you should pay attention to any recommendations he or she might give concerning diet, smoking, degree of exercise, and general lifestyle.

Graduated exercise programs of the kind popularized by *reputable* health clubs across the nation have definite merit. They measure your pulse rate after fixed work loads, and help monitor your exercise so that you do not attempt too much. However, beware of a number of sham clubs with unqualified staff and lifetime membership deals. Your doctor will be able to refer you to a good facility in your area.

Disorganized exercise, such as sporadic jogging on your own when you are no longer in shape to tolerate it, can be quite dangerous. Sports appealing to the aggressive nature, such as those with direct one-on-one competition— for example, racquetball, tennis, and squash— can be bad if the untrained person is prepared to keep chasing the ball for the sake of winning, at the expense of his or her own exhaustion. Such an approach has all too often resulted in acute heart attacks while on the playing court, especially among Type A personalities. (See Chapter 8.)

If you do exercise on your own, and are not in condition, ask your doctor to show you how to check your pulse properly. Make sure you do not let your pulse rate climb above 180 minus your age until you become quite fit. I suggest counting your wrist or neck pulse for six seconds, then adding a zero. With a high rate, it is easy to lose count if you try to follow it for a full minute.

Daily stretching exercises are also extremely important, and no exercise routine should start off without them. Nothing makes you feel older than waking up with stiff muscles; nothing makes you more vulnerable to injuries than starting into brisk exercises without properly warming up before, and cooling off after. The time to start is today. If you delay these exercises until your retirement years, it is likely that they will not be properly effective, due to tendon changes that come with age.

For children, I recommend sports that can be played for a lifetime, such as skiing, water sports, tennis and other racquet sports, bicycling, jogging, and aerobics. Team contact sports are fine for some kids, but often lead to injuries that can last a lifetime. Also, such sports may be difficult to pursue after a person leaves school and enters the work force. It is much easier for an adult to find one person to play tennis than twenty to play football on short notice.

ALTERNATE STRESSES.
Your score if you have one = +40.
Enter your score here.

Strong Choice Number 5

Realistic Goals—Plus 50 Points

We have seen that unrealistic goals can keep you in a state of perpetual failure by your own marking system. It is important to set clear goals that are realistic for you. Having these established makes it easier for you to attain happiness in your life. Without getting into too much detail, let's just say that proper goal setting involves, at the very least, getting to know yourself well. See Appendix A to find out what social-style quadrant you fit into best. If you like applause and contact with people, you'll obviously not find happiness working with a machine in a back room for the rest of your life. Similarly, if you have a more analytical personality and do not find it rewarding to work directly with the public, it would behoove you to pursue career opportunities that lead in your direction.

Realistic financial goals are also important to your happiness. In deciding what assets you wish to own, it is usually better to *underestimate* rather than *overestimate* your potential earnings. You should also decide how much time you wish to spend at work, and how much time you wish to devote to your personal life with family and friends. It might be possible to work around the clock to make enough money to retire after ten years, but it is difficult to do this without alienating family and friends (not to mention paying alimony). The thing to do is to set out a *timetable* that is realistic, as well as identifying the *goals* that you wish to attain. Assess where you would like to be in one, three, and five years' time. If you are realistic, you will have a far greater chance of resisting the effects of stress.

REALISTIC GOALS.
Your score if you
have them = +50.
Enter your score here.

Strong Choice Number 6

Understanding of Stress and Its Effects— Plus 60 Points

Conscious Competence

Once you have finished this book, you will have gained an important advantage in learning to harness stress. This includes knowing your own body, identifying the stresses around you, and learning correct ways to manage stress. With this sort of understanding, you have one of the best possible weapons of defense. Without it, you could well blunder into a premature grave, quite by accident. Of course, there is no point in having this understanding if you don't apply it. This is why it is useful to have friends and family who also understand principles of stress management, and can help you get back "on track" if you stray.

Back in the 1930s, the life-threatening habit of cigarette smoking was not seen as such but was regarded as quite harmless. Cigarettes were simple movie props that suggested poise and thus claimed many unsuspecting victims. Today, however, with proper *knowledge*, you can avoid the ill health and possible premature death that attend the cigarette smoking habit. Similarly, we have now identified many other enemies just as clearly, as you have already read in this book. With an increased understanding of the pitfalls, you can avoid them.

UNDERSTANDING OF STRESS. Your score if you have it = +60. Enter your score here.

Strong Choice Number 7

Relaxation Skills and Efficient Sleep— Plus 70 Points

Can you *relax* when under pressure? If not, learn how to take a quick *"power nap."*

If your job involves a lot of reading, it would make sense to learn to speed-read. If your life contains a lot of stress, it would be a tremendous help to be able to take a quick "power nap" for even a few moments when under fire. Most people can relax on a two-week vacation, many can totally relax on the weekend, and some can relax every evening after work. But how many, during even the most stressful days, can count to ten, suddenly be at complete rest for a few moments, and then wake up refreshed? This is the *power nap*, and I will show you how to do it.

This does not mean you will necessarily put yourself sound asleep in the middle of the day, but simply that you can learn to slow your pulse and breathing rate, and reverse many of the natural stress responses in your body. Depending on the images or triggers that are designed for you, you could, for example, count to ten and place yourself on a nice beach with your hand in the warm sand for a few seconds. Then you could count back down to zero and be fully refreshed. Other people find success by closing their eyes for a few seconds and imagining a dial, set on *high,* when they are very tense. In their minds, they simply imagine the dial being turned down. In this way, they can gain control of themselves, and "command" their pulse and blood pressure rates to decrease.

Some of you already have skills to help you relax on command, gained from such diverse (and excellent) activities as prayer, yoga, martial arts, meditation, exercise, listening to music, and doing favorite odd jobs around the house. But if you find that your current levels of stress are too high for even these methods, then you should have an ace up your sleeve: the *power nap.*

Best learned with a few lessons from your own hypnotist, the *power nap* can be taken at the drop of a hat. It can break up your most stressful days with a few moments of total relaxation for your body (to the extent that you will be unable to prevent your jaw from slackening). It also relaxes your mind (so that you are aware of none of your surrounding stresses). With practice and coaching, you may be able to gain an excellent recharging of your batteries in a few minutes per day, and spare yourself the burnout of the constant use of the same brain and body circuits. The same skills are also helpful in getting to sleep at night.

Efficient sleep

As discussed earlier, efficient sleep is crucial. By this, we do not mean that you necessarily require eight hours a night, but rather that you should have as many hours as you need to perform your day's activities well. Your sleeping hours, ideally, should be consecutive, but many people do well on shorter power naps during the day. Whatever the style and duration, an efficient sleep is of tremendous importance in terms of improving your resistance to stress. If you are one of those lucky people who need only four or five hours per night, consider this a gift of extra time added to your life, and make use of it. Don't waste it just lying in bed trying to pretend you are still asleep.

RELAXATION SKILLS AND EFFICIENT SLEEP. Your score if you have them = +70. Enter your score here.

How to take a power nap

Many people have unfounded fears of hypnosis, and worry that they will lose control of their minds—rather like being on drugs.

In fact, hypnosis is not only harmless, but will help you to *gain* control of your mind. It can be used to great advantage when under stress.

The following is a typical example of what you might expect to hear when a professional is guiding you into hypnosis:

Just sit back and make yourself comfortable and allow your eyelids to close . . .

As you listen to my voice, you can pay attention to the growing feelings of relaxation and comfort in your body . . .

I am going to count for you from one to ten . . .

and as I do . . .

you can imagine yourself traveling down in an elevator to a private place of peace and tranquility . . .

one . . .

just beginning . . .

letting relaxation spread through your scalp . . .

and your face . . .

and your neck . . .

two . . .

going down deeper . . .

more relaxed . . .

down to tranquility . . .

three . . .

arms and hands relaxing . . .

breathing easy . . .

four . . .

every breath guiding you to deeper relaxation . . .

closer to your special place . . .

free from stress and tension . . .

five . . .

down the elevator . . .

stomach knots dissolving . . .

deeper relaxation . . .

calm . . .

comfortable . . .

six . . .

deeper still . . .

letting go of all cares and worries . . .

buttocks and thighs relaxing now . . .

relaxing deeply . . .

seven . . .

legs and feet joining in the growing relaxation . . .

all the way down . . .

to the tips of your toes . . .

eight . . .

journeying deeper . . .

to your special private place . . .

totally calm . . .
more profoundly relaxed . . .
nine . . .
almost there . . .
drifting comfortably deeper . . .
ten . . .
letting the elevator doors open . . .
step out into your place of calmness and
freedom from stress . . .
enjoy the feelings . . .
let them soak deep into every part of you . . .
just let yourself drift with these feelings for a
short while . . .
and when you're ready . . .
just come back up this elevator in your own
way . . .
and bring these calm feelings with you . . .
all the way back to your everyday state of
alertness . . .
*refreshed and relaxed . . . ***

In order to experience this more fully, try The Joy of Stress Power Nap audiocasssette (see p. 279). An original, soothing music score on side one aids relaxation. Once this ideal state has been mastered, you will be challenged on side two by increasingly annoying common distractions. After practicing these "stress rehearsals" for the theater-of-the-real a few times in your home, you will be able to control your *response* even when you can't always control the stress.

---

*Courtesy of Dr. Steven Crainford, Hypnotherapy Associates, Toronto, Canada.

Ways to fall asleep

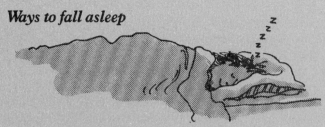

1. Try and go to bed at the same time each night, preferably about half an hour before you plan to fall asleep.
2. Never use your bed as a desk. If you have paper work to be done, sit up at a proper table. Forcing yourself to stay alert while lying on your bed reinforces bad sleeping habits.
3. Have a warm drink (not alcoholic or with caffeine) at bedtime—hot milk is excellent. A relaxing warm bath can also help.
4. Leave your work problems at work; leave your home problems at the bedroom door.
5. Invest in a good quality comfortable mattress. (Try all kinds, including waterbeds, before deciding.) A mattress covering of real sheepskins can also upgrade the comfort of most beds. Comfortable pillows, such as down, and duvets or quilts can also help.
6. Your bedroom should be quiet in both noise levels and decoration.
7. Use your "power nap" relaxation techniques to slow your breathing and pulse rates, and help get you off to sleep. (See page 94.)
8. Strive for "success" in responding to stress. As you approach excellence in your body and stress management, you will be able to sleep more easily. See Chapter 9 for more information on how to achieve success.

BEWARE: There can be hazards in self-hypnosis

OO, LA, LA!

Recently I was flying to Monte Carlo on Air France to give a lecture on stress. The plane was full of people from the North American business community, most of whom would be attending my lecture. I was wedged between a bereaved French widow and my wife, who was eight months pregnant. I spent the first three hours of the flight alternately consoling my wife and the widow. Finally, with only two hours left before arriving in Paris, they both fell asleep. That left me one of the few people still wide awake on the darkened plane.

However, I was confident in the knowledge that I had a plan. One week prior to flight time, I had had a colleague hypnotize me, and make a tape recording while he did it. (My wife had noted two practical problems when I used the tape to get to sleep: I snored, and I twitched my limbs like an egg beater.)

I inserted my glass of ice water into its plastic ring on the back of the seat in front of me. With a sly grin, I then pulled out my secret "weapons": the hypnosis tape and a headphone. I turned it on, and was soon in the deepest of sleeps.

Ten minutes later, however, I awoke, sitting in a cold puddle of water. In my sleep, I had twitched my right knee and inverted the glass of water. In the process, I had managed to spill quite a bit into the lap of my French seatmate. She leapt up with a start, shrieking, "Douche! Douche!" (French for *shower,* but with a rather unfortunate connotation in English).

I quickly tried to make amends by brushing off her wet dress and raining apologies on her. When she calmed down, I grabbed the nearest newspaper and whisked myself up to the toilet, holding the paper strategically over the dark water stains on the worst areas of my light gray pants. Alternating sides, I held the paper so that it was facing toward whoever was awake in either aisle seat.

There was a smallish lineup along each aisle for the two toilets in our section. I stood in the shadows until my turn came, then bolted for the door, breathing a quick sigh of relief. Help, however, was not to be easily found. Paper towels simply wouldn't do the drying job fast enough. Through sheer ingenuity born of stress, I quickly took off my pants and stood up on the toilet seat to hold the wet areas under the rather meager stream of air from the overhead swivel jet.

After at least forty minutes, I went to put my trousers on and noted to my horror that my boxer shorts were still wringing wet. (I had packed all my sensible shorts. The ones I had on were white with large red hearts—the amusing gift of an old girlfriend.)

So, with trousers over the arm, and large red hearts over my head, I again took my perch atop the toilet seat, my back to the door.

Suddenly the lights dimmed as the door flew open to the anguished cry of a now large and irate lineup of passengers with full bladders. Eyes bulged as they were greeted by what could only be described as a "Moon over the Coast of France, with Hearts." Braying several excuses about the poor quality of ventilation in French airplane lavatories, I quickly reclosed the door. Then I got dressed and minced back to my seat, pretending to be deeply engrossed in current events with my nose buried in the open newspaper. I arrived in Paris totally exhausted.

Strong Choice Number 8
Thorough Job Preparation—Plus 80 Points

... I AM FLATTERED TO HAVE BEEN INVITED TO SPEAK TO SUCH A DISTINGUISHED AUDIENCE TODAY...

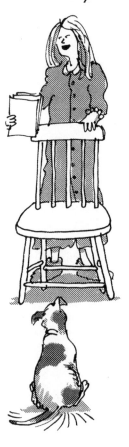

Thorough job preparation is most important to the withstanding of stress. Ideally, in the right job, you should be at your level of competence, with all the appropriate skills. You should know where you are on your stress curve (see page xx) to know if you need to say "yes" to more extra-curricular activities to increase your efficiency; or say "no" to added duties to avoid the inefficiency of too much stress.

This, combined with up-to-the-minute, thorough preparation for that day's tasks, gives you a much better ability to resist the stresses of those tasks. If you are properly prepared for the job, you will derive a much greater joy from it, just as a dress rehearsal improves the opening night show. In just the same way, a "stress rehearsal" will help you handle your daily challenges. By way of further illustration, just think of the different stress levels of students when writing final exams. Those who are ill-prepared sweat bullets; those who have studied well actually enjoy the stress.

Thorough preparation can also be augmented by developing skills of positive imaging. This has been shown to great advantage in the field of sports. For example, showing a high jumper a series of film clips of his or her best jumps will help to erase bad habits (manifested in failed jumps) without even mentioning them.

A recent study divided basketball players into three groups. One group practiced their free throws. The next group did exactly the same thing at the other end, but in pantomime, *without the ball.* The third group spent its time sitting on the sidelines. Predictably, the last group did not show any improvement. The amazing thing was that the first two groups showed equal improvement, thus indicating that even in your imagination, and without a ball, you can still gain thorough job preparation. This same sort of imaging applies to every sport, as well as every job. For example, if you have a speech to give, you can often have as productive a rehearsal in your mind as in a dry run.

THOROUGH JOB PREPARATION.
Your score if you have it = +80.
Enter your score here.

Strong Choice Number 9

Financial Security—Plus 90 Points

It is not necessary to have vast riches to qualify here. What we are talking about is having enough financial security (in the form of positive cash flow, assets, skills, or insurance policies) to avoid being thrown out on the street if you lose your job through changes in your health, or in the economy. This will give you a crucial "control button" to fight stress.

On a daily basis, if all your loans can be consolidated into a manageable repayment program and if your current spending habits are within your *net* means, then you will be in an excellent position to withstand stresses.

No matter what your salary level, you should have a written budget, and allow some money for *stress defense*. This need not cost a lot: it could be as simple as going to the movies regularly, or hiring a young student to help with some chores around the house. The important thing is to spend this money regularly, and in advance *before* you finally see your health suffer from excess stress. *Pamper yourself.* (See Chapter 10.)

A preplanned miniholiday each month is much more valuable than one taken after a whole year of uninterrupted stress. Write out your priorities, list the stresses that bother you most, and coordinate solutions within the limits of your budget.

If your time at work is valuable, it may pay you to hire out all the household chores you can afford (saving only those that give you *leisure* while you work). If you will lose money by not arriving back at the office promptly on Monday morning, then a confirmed airline seat is a better investment than a cheap standby ticket for your holiday. If you do a lot of driving at work, then invest in the most comfortable and appealing car that you can afford. Or do as I have done and hire a student to drive you to work, thus giving you a gift of extra time to read, dictate, or even rest. Surround yourself with the home that best fulfills your needs, and creature comforts that will soothe your spirits at the end of each working day. But take care do do this *within your budget.* Otherwise you will quickly cross over into the financial mismanagement side, as we have seen in Chapter 3.

FINANCIAL SECURITY.
Your score if you have it = +90.
Enter your score here.

Strong Choice Number 10

Stable Home—Plus 100 Points

This does not mean you have to live in a stable, keep pets, or be married (although the latter two help greatly). But if you invest enough of your energy and time in maintaining an adequate network of friends and support from within your family, the stresses of your day will be greatly reduced. This means you can get away from work pressure daily, which is a more frequent and valuable reward than escaping just once a year for vacation.

It is important to bear in mind that the time and effort involved in maintaining good relationships with family and friends are well worthwhile. If this aspect of your life is working well, you have mastered the most valuable defense you can possibly have against stress. Strong faith in a religion and/or a high code of ethical behavior can also be of tremendous solace. Along with many other factors, this may explain why groups such as Mormons tend to live longer.

Pets have been shown to ease their owners' stresses by decreasing their blood pressure and pulse when they cuddle up for some touching. As a result, their owners tend to live longer. Married people also tend to live longer than single people (although sometimes it just *seems* longer). One common link is that we all need to be touched frequently.

Of course, physical touching is only one aspect of close personal relationships. There are also many psychological, social, and spiritual benefits. An important aspect is to *communicate* at home, to share your burdens of stress. If sacrifices have to be made, then your family will understand, and be behind you. Do not be afraid to broach difficult topics. By building up the negative consequences of problems to the point of silent paralysis, you can destroy a good relationship. Emphasize the strong positive benefits of sharing your stresses, and difficult topics become much easier to broach and solve.

STABLE HOME.
Your score if you have it = +100.
Enter your score here.

How did you do?

STRONG CHOICES	POSSIBLE SCORE	ENTER YOUR SCORE
1. Good Genetics	+10	
2. Sense of Humor	+20	
3. Right Diet	+30	
4. Alternate Exercise	+40	
5. Realistic Goals	+50	
6. Understanding of Stress	+60	
7. Relaxation Skills and Efficient Sleep	+70	
8. Thorough Job Preparation	+80	
9. Financial Security	+90	
10. Stable Home	+100	
Total score if you made all the right choices = +550 **YOUR TOTAL**		

Enter your score from preceding page.

☐ *Strong Choices*

Next, enter your total score from the weak choices at the end of the last chapter (see page 74).

☐ *Weak Choices*

Now add these two numbers to give you your net resistance to stress.

☐ *Hanson Stress Resistance*

Finally, subtract your Holmes-Rahe stress score (see page 49.)

☐ *Holmes-Rahe Stress Level*

This will give you your grand total, your net stress score.

☐ *Net Stress Score*

A score of more than –300 = an *80 percent chance of serious change in your health. Consult your doctor soon!*

Now we can get a realistic picture of your true risks from stress. The higher your net score (in a positive direction), the better you are doing at harnessing your stresses, and the less likely you will be to have any serious heart attacks, ulcers, or other health crises or to cause inefficiencies at work.

With a negative score (in excess of –300), your risks are deadly serious. Note that even with no recent stresses on the Holmes-Rahe scale, you could still be in the high risk group just based on your weak choices on the Hanson Scale of Stress Resistance.

It's *your choice*. Bankruptcy, poor health, and early death from stress are only rarely due to true bad luck; usually it is due to *incompetence* (albeit unconscious). Note that in badly run companies the effects of incompetence can be passed down through the hierarchy, thus multiplying its devastation. After reading this book, you should be able to actively choose to *strengthen* yourself in response to stress—in other words, live longer and better by *conscious competence*.

Remember, even if you score well today, stress is dynamic. Review your position on the scale often. If you are a manager of people, have your employees review their levels on a regular basis.

5.
Nutrition and Stress

Seldom has so much been written about so little as in the field of nutrition. The subject is very much in vogue in all of the media today. The jargon of nutrition is complex—guaranteed to include words beyond the understanding of all but the Ph.D. biochemist. Impressive sounding though such words may be, the truth is that the subject of nutrition is not a terribly difficult one at all. In fact, before the Industrial Revolution, when the science of nutrition was almost totally undeveloped, people probably ate a better diet than we do now with all our sophisticated knowledge of the subject.

If you have symptoms of ill health, you need a *diagnosis* before you need a diet or nutritional counseling. Once the diagnosis has been made, your doctor will *then* send you to the appropriate nutrition professional for specific advice if needed. This is the way the diet for a diabetic is chosen. The same is true for advice to post-heart attack patients, the obese, fatigued, anorectic, and so on.

An old professor of mine used to say that most people would improve their diet if they ate shredded cellophane sprinkled with essential amino acids. Of course, this rather unappetizing prospect is not meant to be taken literally.

The elements of a good, balanced diet can be divided into the following six categories:

1. *Protein.* 15-20 percent of total calories.
2. *Fats.* 30-35 percent of total calories.
3. *Carbohydrates.* 50 percent of total calories.
4. *Fiber.* 50 grams per day (see appendix).
5. *Vitamins and Minerals.* *
6. *Water.* Eight glasses per day.

Precise measurements of your foods are not necessary. Listed percentages of the first three elements can easily be "eyeballed" by having them in proportion on your plate. Consult your doctor or public health office for standard recommended balanced diet sheets. * *

Obesity, which is rampant in all age groups in this country, does not necessarily mean that too much fat and carbohydrate have been consumed; it means that too many calories (of *any* sort of food) have been consumed relative to the calories burned off.

Let's take a closer look at the six categories to be included in a balanced diet.

1. Protein

Protein is necessary for our bodies to function. It is also essential for growth. Protein forms the genes that are present right from conception. Protein also gives us antibodies to fight disease. It forms the microscopic enzymes that regulate all body functions. And it makes up much of our bones, muscles, organs, bloodstream, and hormones.

A separate section is devoted to the important subject of vitamins and minerals. (See appendix.)

* *Examples of a balanced diet may be seen in the appendix.*

Everyone recognizes the importance of protein, but unfortunately many tend to overdo it. The typical North American diet has far more protein than required. Protein is found in most foods, not just meats.

Excess protein in the diet will be converted to fat, as will excesses of any foods. Excess protein is also excreted—as nitrogen waste. The added "work" of having to eliminate it may cause harm to people suffering liver or kidney disease.

A chronic excess of dietary protein may result in decreased calcium, resulting in demineralization of bones. Thus it is important that protein be taken in sensible amounts, approximately 15-20 percent of your total calories.

2. Fats

Fats are not actually "bad," but have been abused in our diets. They often form almost 45 percent of our calories, when two-thirds of this amount would suffice. A balanced diet should include both animal and vegetable fats, making up 30 to 35 percent of your total calories. Over-reacting, trying to keep the fat intake near zero is *not* the answer. Some authorities, such as the late Dr. Nathan Pritikin, have noted that heart disease is extremely rare in Third World communities with a meatless and fat-free diet. However, this shows the dangers of drawing conclusions by looking at only one organ in the body. While it is true that these people developed little heart disease, most of them didn't live long enough to enjoy this fact. Their total life span was remarkably *shorter* than ours. Their rate of maternal and infant mortality was

very high, and the death rate from what should have been easily defendable infections was appalling, because of their malnutrition.

The American Heart Association has pointed out that fats are essential building blocks of our vital immune and defense systems, and should *not* be kept to zero intake.

Recently there has been a lot of public alarm about the high incidence of cholesterol in the coronary arteries of heart attack victims. Studies have concluded that this must be due to our relatively high cholesterol diet. Autopsies on young (eighteen-year-old) soldiers in the Korean War showed that the American boys had cholesterol placques already clogging up their arteries, while the Chinese and Korean boys did not. Two glaring differences between the cultures were the high fat diet versus the rice diet, and the levels of serum cholesterols. In the U.S. these were 50 percent higher than the Korean levels.

The initial reaction was to blame only *ingested* cholesterol for the *deposited* cholesterol. However, other key factors have since been identified:

Fiber

(See page 121). This is found only in plant materials; it acts as a passive sponge, just visiting your intestines and not entering the rest of your body. If taken in adequate amounts (50 grams per day), it will carry out four times the average amount of stool each day. Stools get their brown color from bile salts, which are made by your own liver, and are rich in cholesterol (even if you are a total vegetarian). These bile salts are

resorbed into the bloodstream if not carried
out in stool. Thus, if a person eats more
fiber, and quadruples the amount of stool,
the blood levels of cholesterol are bound to
decline. (The Korean diet was high in
fiber; the American diet at that time was
low in fiber.)

Excess stress

If you choose to make yourself *weaker* in
response to stress (see Chapter 3) and build
up 300 points against yourself on the stress
scale, then you will probably suffer the
same deposits of cholesterol in the arteries
that befell all of Hans Selye's stressed rats.
In Western society, fighting the time clock,
both on the assembly line and with office
deadlines, is a big stress factor that appears
to remove any possibility of control from
the hands of the individual. (As we will see
in Chapter 10, this is not necessarily
irrevocable.)

Korean society at the time of the Korean
War was slower, based on rural agriculture. The
passage of time was measured by the season
rather than by the millisecond. Levels of Net
Stress score were much lower, primarily
because the Hanson Resistance score was
higher. This would tend to help keep the
arteries of the Koreans freer of deposits of cholesterol than those of their U.S. counterparts.

The major role of fat is that of energy storage. Fat has nine calories per gram, whereas
proteins and carbohydrates store only four calories per gram. Therefore, when a diet is high in
fat, it is extremely easy to consume too many
calories, without taking up much space in your

CALORIE STORAGE

stomach. Fats can be easily hidden in foods and in the cooking process. Many people are aware of animal fats, such as are visible in meats, gravy, chicken skin, and so on. But they forget that vegetable fats have just as many calories. The typical two-piece fried chicken dinner with French fries can have over one thousand calories because of the fats used in frying. A serving of French fries with gravy can have as much as eight hundred calories.

Besides energy storage, fat does also play other roles in the body. It cushions organs such as the kidneys, and acts as a storehouse for fat-soluble vitamins (A, D, E, and K). Another lesser function of fat is insulation in the wintertime.

The cholesterol (blood) test

A complete serum lipid profile should be done every three years if you are under stress. You should make your doctor aware of the stresses that you are facing. Otherwise this test may not be part of his or her routine physical checkup. This test must be done after fasting for at least fourteen hours.

It is not good enough to just test the cholesterol to predict risk of heart disease. A complete lipid profile, including the levels of "good" and "bad" forms of cholesterol, and an indexing or "typing" should also be done. Certain familial types of high cholesterol, once identified, can be important to check in all your blood relatives, including children over the age of ten.

What to do if your doctor tells you your cholesterol is high.

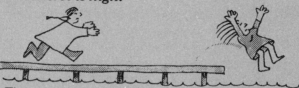

There are six steps to its reduction:

1. Lose weight if obese, and return to your ideal body weight.

2. Reduce total dietary intake of fats including animal fats. After a trial period, your doctor will want to review your progress and reassess dietary advice.

3. Increase dietary fiber to 50 grams per day (see appendix). Fiber acts like a sponge to increase the volume of stool from a quarter pound to one pound per day. This quadruples the amount of endogenously produced cholesterol that you excrete per day.

4. Do regular exercise (after medical and fitness consultations). Cholesterol is just a fuel, and if you do more exercise, some of it will naturally be burned up.

5. Take steps to correct *excess stresses*. If your life is getting too complicated, pause to reflect upon ways to simplify it. Are you running too fast just because everyone else is, or are you truly happy in your work and relationships with others? Reduce unnecessary controllable stresses, such as type A behavior. Use the Hanson Scale of Stress Resistance to improve your resistance to those stresses you cannot control.

6. Only as a last resort, you may wish to discuss the role of drug therapy with your doctor.

Butter versus margarine

Because of the public awareness of cholesterol deposits in the arteries in connection with heart disease, many people have erroneously come to think of margarine as a "health food," and butter as being "bad for you."

Many other factors are involved in heart disease. The extent to which ingested cholesterol causes deposited cholesterol is not clearly defined, and is still under investigation.

Many of the cheaper brands of margarine are actually *high* in saturated fats. If you wish to reduce your dietary intake of these fats, you must look for a top-quality margarine labeled as having more than 35 percent polyunsaturates.

Margarine, however, is not a "health" food, nor is it a wonder drug. It is just a food, as is butter. Margarine may be included in the dietary recommendations if your doctor discovers that you have a problem (see page 115), and tries you on a diet restricted in saturated fat.

Following a repeat test, your doctor will assess whether it makes any difference in your blood levels. If successful, then he or she might suggest continuing to reduce dietary polyunsaturates. If the blood levels do not decline significantly, the doctor might well suggest that it would be pointless to change your usual (balanced) diet.

Margarine is also recommended for those who don't have access to refrigeration (for example, people on camping trips), and those suffering from allergies to dairy products.

Caution: Some margarines may contain skim milk powder. Check the label carefully.

Margarine does have a large number of food additives in it and, to many people, tastes inferior to butter. Margarine has exactly the same number of calories as butter. You will put on just as much fat if you overeat either one. As mentioned earlier, the average diet contains too much fat, and the principle of reducing fat intake to the recommended levels of 30-35 percent (divided between polyunsaturated and saturated) should be endorsed.

The areas of reduction of fats are entirely a matter of personal choice, but there is no need to make sacrifices in taste. Because many people either prefer the taste of butter as a spread, or in cooking, I suggest that you use it if you like it. It should be used on high-fiber bread, or in a high-fiber diet, in keeping with our suggested balance of dietary elements (see page 110).

Reductions in fat intake, in general, can more easily be made by restricting *hidden fats;* for example, by broiling or baking instead of frying, trimming visible fats from meats, and avoiding gravy. Other ways of restricting hidden fats are by having more frequent servings of vegetables, poultry (without the skin), and white fish main courses; and by using corn and safflower oils in salads and dressings.

Studies have shown that Seventh-Day Adventist men between the ages of 35 and 64 have half the risk of a fatal heart attack that the overall population has. This can be explained by the Seventh-Day Adventists' emphasis on strong choices on the Hanson Scale of Stress Resistance, for example, balanced diet (which includes adequate fiber); abstinence from alcohol, cigarettes, and caffeine; and the high value placed on a stable base at home.

In conclusion, fats, both animal and vegetable, can safely make up 30-35 percent of your balanced diet, as long as you eat *enough fiber,* choose a good lifestyle with correct responses to stress, and have normal blood tests.

3. Carbohydrates

These are often viewed as being very fattening. However, carbohydrates have only four calories per gram, which is exactly the same calorie content as protein. There are two kinds of carbohydrates: complex and simple. *Complex* carbohydrates are found in whole foods; for example, wheat, beans, grains, fruits, vegetables. These starches are a very efficient source of energy, and are particularly valuable when you are under stress.

Simple carbohydrates are found in refined sugar, white flour, and alcohol. These are truly empty calories. In the refining process, most traces of fiber are removed. It is excesses of foods such as these, which typically form over 20 percent of the daily American calorie intake, that give carbohydrates a bad name.

This explains why carbohydrates have gained a reputation for being fattening without being filling. Under stress, the level of simple blood sugar is already elevated. Thus the additional ingestion of excesses of simple carbohydrates is redundant.

Figure 5.1

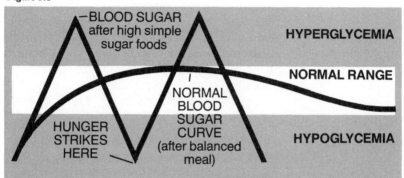

Complex carbohydrates or sugars with fiber, tend to be absorbed much more slowly than refined sugars.

A high level of refined sugar in your diet means that you will be a slave to your sugar graph. You will start out in a hunger crisis from low blood sugar, eat sugar, and then get hyperglycemic with a quickly passing feeling of "fullness." Very shortly thereafter, you will become hypoglycemic, and then have the panic rush for a "quick energy fix." You can't wait for regular foods to gently raise your blood sugar; therefore, you head for more sugar. This can be extremely habit forming, and explains why most people do not stop at just one cookie from a bag.

Complex carbohydrates (such as pastas, whole wheat bread, whole rice), and not pure protein (such as the traditional pre-game steak), are the most efficient sources of energy for any impending acute stress, both on or off the field of athletic endeavor.

Complex carbohydrates are the cleanest burning and easiest source of energy for your body to assimilate. Natural sugar cane (a complex carbohydrate) is actually high in fiber, and tends not to be fattening in spite of its sweetness. Because of the high quality of fiber, natural sugar cane tends to be extremely filling; thus the stomach cannot physically handle an excess amount. "Refined" sugar, on the other hand, has almost all the fiber removed. Thus it is extremely easy to overdo the intake of refined sugar. The average person in North America consumes more than one hundred pounds of sugar per year in various forms. This is several times the required amount.

Sugar is particularly harmful in drinks. A drink with a high sugar content tends to be no more filling than a drink of water. The same size meals can be consumed, whether or not simple sugar has been ingested in drinks during the day. As a general principle, if one takes only those drinks that contain no calories, such as diet sodas, herbal teas, and decaffeinated coffees, then it is much easier to achieve a normal balance in sugar chemistry.

The ideal drink is, of course, water. If the tap water in your area is not drinkable, then a bottle of spring or mineral water will be a good choice. It also goes without saying that it is difficult to become obese if you make a habit of eating your sugar in its original forms; for example, in fruit as opposed to just its juice (which has had the fiber removed).

4. Fiber

Perhaps the most underrated element of our diet is fiber (roughage). This is simply the cell wall material of plant foods, and is not digested by mammals. Thus it cannot be found in any meat, or in animal products such as milk and eggs. One major reason why the Scarsdale Diet is not recommended for any longer than two weeks is that it is unbalanced, providing little in the way of fiber. It can also be harmful to have so much protein, as mentioned in the discussion of metabolism. (However, the Scarsdale Diet is quite safe within its own suggested two-week program.)

Many fad diets based on eating one predominant food, for example, grapefruit, steak, or avocado, are not based on any provable medical evidence. They work simply on the principle of boredom. If you have the same food every day for long enough, you will eventually get sick of it, even if that food was once your favorite.

One of my patients recently admitted to having been on a banana diet for seven weeks. (His weight didn't change, but he now smells like a monkey.)

Fiber is the one food you can eat plenty of, because it does not stay in the body. Eating fiber is something like swallowing a sponge. It passes unchanged through the bowels. Fifty grams of fiber can carry out over one hundred undigested calories in every bowel movement. Thus, if you eat fiber, you can "get away with" eating a bit more food without gaining weight.

Over the past century, modern methods of refining foods have taken more of the fiber out of the average person's diet. At the same time, total sugar consumption has gone from five to one hundred pounds per person per year!

Third World studies have shown that people who eat a lot of fiber have lower rates of heart disease, diabetes, and cancer. They also have fewer disorders of the bowel such as colitis. Dr. Denis Burkitt has noted a strong correlation between these diseases and the size of one's feces. He found that, while the average Western diet produced only one-quarter pound of stool per day, the typical African or Asian diet produced a full pound. The transit time—the time it takes for food ingested to come out the other end in the form of stool—is only one and a half days in Africans. Compare this with the three days taken in the case of most adult North Americans. For our elderly patients, it can be as much as several weeks!

British prisoners of war in Asia during the Second World War ate a diet high in fiber (husks, plant leaves, and so on), while their Japanese guards enjoyed a more refined diet. Even though the prisoners were under greater stress, they had fewer ulcers of the stomach and duodenum than their captors. Some were later transferred to Hong Kong, where they received a more "normal" Western diet. In these prisoners, the rate of ulcers climbed dramatically. When they were returned to more primitive camps, the rate of ulcers went down again.

Many patients initially feel that a high-fiber diet will be unpalatable, such as eating the wrapper off their bran muffin. However, the foods one can eat in this kind of diet may already be among your favorites. They include baked potatoes, whole wheat breads, pasta, sweet corn, peas, and baked beans. You may even be denying yourself these foods in a mis-guided attempt to lose weight. Remember, fiber is extremely filling, and it is (almost) impossible to become severely obese by eating foods that are high in it.

Where can you find fiber? All plants have it, in different forms. Pure wheat bran is about half fiber. Bran is what is left behind during the refining of white flour. It is one of the best forms of fiber, but unfortunately most people find that it tastes a lot like used kitty litter. Since it is difficult to take more than an ounce of bran per day, it is practical to seek out other sources of fiber. (But please don't eat this book!)

It is important to obtain fiber from a variety of foods. In general, vegetables (such as beans, peas, corn), whole grain breads, and high-fiber biscuits are good sources. The following is a list of some specific foods that are high in fiber:

Figure 5.2

FOOD	GRAMS OF FIBER	CALORIES
Baked beans in tomato sauce—1 cup	16.0	180
Baked potato—medium	5.0	91
Raspberries—½ cup	4.6	20
Brown rice—½ cup	5.5	83
High bran health bread—2 slices	7.0	150
Large apple	4.5	80
100% bran cereal—½ cup (1 oz.)	8.2	72
Shredded wheat—2 large biscuits	4.4	190
Bran muffin, with whole wheat flour—no raisins or dates	2.3	78
Fibermed® cookies—2	10.0	120

In the intestine, the "sponge" action of fiber can slow down the rate of absorption of sugar into the bloodstream. This effect can significantly reduce insulin requirements for diabetics. As we have seen, a high-fiber diet can also help to reduce one's blood levels of cholesterol. For dieters, one of the most pleasing side effects of high-fiber consumption is that as much as 10 percent of the total calorie intake, or about 150 calories, will be passed undigested through the body in the form of bowel movements.

Benefits of fiber

In the mouth.

Fiber slows your rate of eating, simply by giving you more volume to chew through for the same number of calories. The obese tend to eat quickly.

Similarly, they often seek diets that will cause them to lose weight quickly. *Fast* seems to be their watchword in both endeavors. The reason for eating quickly could be a sense of panic at not having enough hours in the day to take in the extra few thousand calories they are planning on eating. Alternatively, it could be a misplaced sense of guilt, a fear that someone will catch them eating. The old "hand is quicker than the eye" theory is operating here.

By increasing your fiber and thus having more volume to chew through, you will tend to eat more slowly. Certainly you will feel satisfied longer. Also, more saliva will be stimulated. This aids in the preliminary breakdown of proteins, and improves digestion.

In the stomach.

A high-fiber load slows the stomach's rate of emptying. This means that, instead of being hungry an hour after a meal, your stomach will stay full for several hours. It also means that your stomach acid has more work to do, and tends to burn itself out. This is a natural protective device that is all the more important under stress. When the increased cortisone produced under stress makes the stomach lining vulnerable to its own acid, this is one of the few concrete steps you can take to protect yourself.

In the blood.

Rebound hunger (hypoglycemia) following ingestion of carbohydrate loads lacking fiber has already been discussed. (See figure 5.1.) This is why the traditional tendency to feel hungry an hour after a meal of Chinese food (often composed heavily of white rice) has some basis in medical fact. In point of fact, people in China who live in rural areas do not have white "refined" rice. Their high-fiber rice keeps them full for many hours after a meal.

Initially, after a meal, *insulin* is stimulated in great amounts. Blood sugar stays normal for about two hours, following which there is a rebound phenomenon of hunger. This can be prevented by eating lots of fiber, which slows down digestion of the carbohydrates.

In the intestines.

Eating plenty of fiber means that more calories will be lost in the stool from undigested foods. More protein and cholesterol will also be carried out of the body, in the form of digestive juices that are poured into the intestine to process the food.

It has been shown that the incidence of bowel inflammations (colitis and so on) and, most importantly, bowel cancer is directly related to the amount of fiber present in the diet. Although fiber increases the transit time in the stomach, it decreases the transit time dramatically in the large intestine.

One thing to remember, however, is that calcium absorption can be impaired by a high-fiber diet. This is easily overcome by taking a couple of glasses of milk a day. Alternatively, other foods containing calcium can be taken.

Zinc, magnesium, and other trace elements can also be bound to the fiber. For this reason, supplementation with a daily multiple vitamin pill is also recommended, as we will see shortly.

Constipation: the sure cure

"Constipation" means protracted effort to produce hard, dry stool. The interval between stools is less important than their consistency, and the freedom from discomfort. Constipation is one of the most common problems that I see, particularly in the elderly. It is also, surprisingly, a problem in many younger people, often resulting from simple inactivity. While constipation may seem to be a lifelong problem, and a disease that knows no cure, nothing could be further from the truth. Constipation is not a disease; it is simply a preventable malfunction or a "disorganization."

There are three simple steps to follow in correcting constipation:

1. Eat enough fiber in your diet.

Aim for 50 grams per day, from foods. Consult Appendix C for more information. Fiber supplements are certainly safe, but should be redundant if you eat properly.

The old axiom, "An apple a day keeps the doctor away," originated primarily from the fact that an apple provides fiber, which helps prevent constipation.

2. Correct stomach muscle tone.

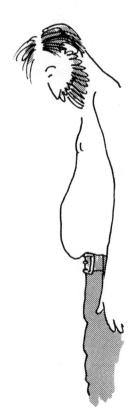

Having adequate stomach muscle tone is crucial to avoiding constipation; it increases pressure on the intestine walls. This is why even perfectly healthy young athletes may require something for their bowels when confined for extended periods to a hospital bed. Muscles are little used during bed rest, and consequently lose their tone. This is also true during pregnancy and the postpartum state.

As far as the elderly are concerned, stomach muscle tone presents a major problem in many cases, as the stomach muscles may not have had a good workout ever—or certainly not in the last few years. Because more of today's elderly are women (for historical reasons discussed elsewhere in this book), and because they lived through a time when girdles and corsets were used as substitutes for aerobic exercises, the problem of constipation seems to be worse with women. In particular, it seems to be worse with women who are obese.

However, the problem can affect any age or either sex if the abdominal wall muscles are slack. I have seen a surprising degree of constipation from lazy stomach muscles, even in children.

3. Timing.

Although it sounds rather distasteful, there is an aptly named medical function in your body known as the gastro-colic "dumping" reflex. This reflex occurs about twenty minutes after filling the stomach with a large meal, and is your cue to have a bowel movement. In many cases the reflex takes place while you are on a bus, in a meeting, or otherwise in a bad spot to act upon it. If you wait till a couple of hours after a meal to go to the bathroom, you lose the natural advantage of this reflex, and generally have less success.

Incorporating the above information, the simplest plan is to select a time during the day that is practical for you, such as breakfast. Start off your morning twenty minutes earlier than usual, which should allow you time to do some stomach exercises and general stretching exercises. Then have your breakfast, which should be high in fiber and fluid volume; for example, whole wheat toast, bran cereal, fresh fruit, and a glass or two of your favorite bottled water. Make sure your schedule allows you to spend five minutes or so on the toilet when you get the "call of the sphincter" after breakfast.

I have never seen this plan fail for anybody, if adhered to on a regular basis. There is virtually no need to take any of the commercially available drugs. Constipation, as we have seen, is not a disease, but a disorganization.

One other cure for constipation has emerged from the ancient Chinese art of acupuncture. There is one needle six inches long, which may work if all else fails. The doctor does not need to insert this needle into the skin. All that's necessary is to show it to the patient!

Here are three examples of safe, effective stomach exercises. For more details, consult your doctor and fitness professional.

One of the best diet tips is to keep most of your liquids calorie-free. Otherwise you will drink a lot of empty calories, but not do anything to suppress your appetite for the next meal. In general, avoid fruit juices (which are just the fruit without the fiber), and eat the whole fruit instead. On a hot afternoon it would be quite easy to drink several glasses of apple juice, without having any appetite suppression by dinner time. If you tried to eat all the whole apples that the juice was extracted from, you couldn't finish them, never mind eat your normal sized dinner.

5. Vitamins and Minerals

Much nonsense has been written and claimed about vitamins and minerals. The R.D.A. (Recommended Daily Allowance) of these elements is found in most *balanced* diets.

However, there are cases in which the dietary source alone may be inadequate, such as on the high-fiber regimen that I recommend for stress. The same high-fiber content that protects you from stress can also bind some of the vitamins and minerals to it, thus interfering with their absorption into the bloodstream. This is easily corrected by taking a single multiple vitamin supplement.

Other cases in which dietary sources of vitamins and minerals may prove inadequate include:

• A strict vegetarian diet.
• Dieting for obesity; in effect, eating fewer than 1,500 calories per day.
• Pregnancy and lactation.
• Growth during childhood.
• Poor absorption in the elderly.
• Alcohol and drug addiction.
• Recovery from surgery, burns, or illness.
• Being under excessive stress.

It is important to consult with your doctor about taking vitamins. Taking megavitamins can be not only harmful if unsupervised, but even fatal. Furthermore, just because it is claimed that a vitamin is "organic" does not mean that taking the whole alphabet is harmless, or that the organic vitamin is inherently better than a regular one. In fact, shelf life and stability of organic vitamins are often worse than for regular vitamins.

The chart in Appendix B, at the end of this book, gives some basic facts about vitamins and minerals. This chart is provided only for the sake of reference and completeness. Though it may sometimes seem so, the subject of vitamins and minerals is not really a complicated one.

Vitamin jargon fluently quoted by "experts" (including not only lay nutritionists, but some members of the medical profession) can falsely impress the public. People can easily find relevance to themselves in the vague and general nature of the symptoms cited for dietary deficiencies.

6. *Water*

I recommend (and drink) eight glasses of water per day. This is particularly important for anyone experiencing a lot of stress. Adequate water consumption will benefit many areas of the body.

1. The bloodstream

Eight glasses of water per day offer a protective dilutant effect. As we have seen in Chapter 2, one of the body's reflex responses to stress is to thicken the blood with extra clotting factors and red blood cells, both from the marrow and from the reservoir of the spleen. Having this "sludge" effect in your arteries can compromise the circulation and, in coronary vessels already partly occluded with early heart disease, predispose you to a heart attack. For the same reasons, emboli (blood clots traveling through the vessels, which get lodged in other organs) and strokes can also be encouraged by not drinking enough water.

The effects of taking medication to thin the blood prophylactically are still being studied. Current findings suggest it is better not to medicate young adults routinely, as the long-term side effects of several decades of drug use in humans are not sufficiently known. However, it *is* known that dehydration thickens the blood, and hydration thins it. Thus the simple addition of eight glasses of water to your daily diet can offer real benefits in your defense against stress.

2. The skin

The skin has more wrinkles and roughness
when the body is dehydrated. Also, the skin
needs adequate supplies of water to regulate
body temperature through sweating.

3. The gastro-intestinal tract

Good hydration assists in digestion, and in
passing of soft stools.

Water pills are popular because of the prompt loss
of up to five or six pounds of fluid in the first few
days. As a result, they are increasingly being
sought by dieters. However, as I explain to people,
"water pills" are misnamed, and would more correctly be labeled "salt-losing pills." Wherever the
salt goes, water will follow passively; thus it makes
little sense to take a pill to lose salt through your
urine if you continue to take in extra salt in your
meals. If you restrict your water intake, your blood
gets saltier, and you thus retain even more water.
The same benefit as obtained through these
diuretics can usually be obtained by salt restriction
and extra water consumption. This approach is far
safer, since it does not pose risks to the delicate
balance of electrolytes in your body. In any event,
losing water by whatever means is still irrelevant to
the dieter. What he or she really needs to lose is *fat*.

4. The lungs and nasal passages

In dry or cold air, your lungs act as living *humidifiers* for the surrounding air. The frost you see with each exhaled breath in cold weather is actually just water being lost from your body. The same thing applies to each invisible breath in warm, dry air. The normal mucous lining in the lungs can become very thick and glue-like if the water lost through the lungs is not being matched by water intake. This can lead to a decrease in your resistance against chest infections.

5. The urinary tract

The benefits of good hydration here are many. Maintaining a high volume of urine output helps prevent a host of urinary tract problems, such as stones and infections in the bladder and kidneys. It also keeps the bloodstream washed free of excess waste products from metabolism. Without proper hydration, relative stages of kidney "failure" can occur with serious system-atic consequences, including decreased mental alertness, fatigue, blood pressure elevations, fluid retention, and so on.

In most large urban areas, the water supply is safe and cheap, but is better suited to washing dishes and watering gardens than to drinking in large quantities. When I tell patients to drink their eight glasses of water daily (some of which may come from fluids in other drinks), I find a real problem with compliance. From the prac-tical point of view, I must admit that eight glasses of turbid, chemically treated, metallic tasting tap water is unappetizing. Those who have followed my advice on increasing water intake—but used unfiltered tap water—have often quickly abandoned it after their initial enthusiasm, simply because of the unsavory taste.

The purest water is distilled, but it has absolutely no taste. The tastiest water is natural spring, or mineral water. This is simply rain and melted snow that has filtered through layers of sand and rocks over decades, and collected in deep, clean underground pools. Depending on the nature of the local soil and sand, each spring may have a different mineral content, and thus a different taste. It should be easy for you to find one that appeals to you, and that you will enjoy.

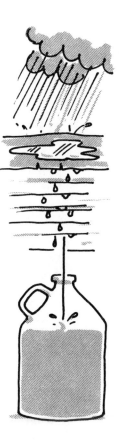

In North America, there has never been any hesitation about buying water, as long as it contained sugar (pop, juices), alcohol (beer, wine), or caffeine (coffee, tea, iced tea). From the point of view of thirst, however, the water alone is all you need. If you view the purchase of your favorite bottled water as a substitute for buying some of these other drinks, you will probably still end up ahead financially, reduce your dental bills, and increase your resistance to stress.

■

A word on salt

Sodium is a vital element in our body chemistry; without it we would die. Historically, it was considered so important that workers were given pieces of rock salt as payment. Interestingly enough, this was the basis for our word *salary.*

Strenuous work or sports in hot weather can increase the body's demands for salt, due to salt loss through sweating. (Ironically, sweat is actually quite low in salt, compared with blood. However, after continued evaporation, a residue of salt is left on the skin, much to the delight of your friendly household dog.)

Salt lost in this way needs to be replaced, but handfuls of salt pills can easily become an overdose. You can make a more accurate replacement by adding one teaspoon of salt to a quart of water with lemon juice. Or, if that sounds a little unappetizing, try one of the premixed fruit and electrolyte drinks commonly seen along the sidelines at sports events. One quart of skim milk per day, along with plenty of water and fruit juice, will also be helpful.

Salt is added in large quantities to many prepared foods as a preservative, and as a teaser promoting the craving to have even *more* salt. (No one eats just *one* salted peanut or potato chip.)

The average person needs three grams of salt per day, or less than two-thirds of a teaspoon. Apart from the above-mentioned special circumstances, salt need *not* be added at the table, in cooking, or via high-salt snack foods. Excesses of salt can aggravate high blood pressure, congestive heart failure, and kidney failure. They can also cause fluid retention (often seen during pregnancy, in premenstrual tension, and in cases of heart failure).

A word on "jet lag"

"Jet lag" is the physiological disorientation of all bodily and mental functions that accompanies flights across several time zones (in other words, only on flights in east/west directions).

This phenomenon is particularly annoying to the frequent business traveler, whose ability to make sharp decisions suffers from traveler's fatigue.

To a certain extent, these physiological changes (mediated by our internal diurnal or twelve-hour "clock") are an unavoidable travel nuisance. However, many of the temptations on the flight will actually make the jet lag worse, such as late night movies, cheap (or free) alcoholic beverages, and large meals, especially if served at an unusual hour for your own internal "clock." Overnight flights further interrupt sleeping.

However a major problem is, surprisingly, dehydration.

In a pressurized aircraft, the ambient humidity during the flight is usually less than 2 percent. The air temperature outside the plane is −40° F. When this air is warmed to room temperature, it becomes extremely dry. The only reason this air has even 2 percent water is because of the warm passengers' bodies. Body water is donated to the air via the skin (which explains the dry skin and mouth after a flight), and, mainly, through the lungs. Every breath gives up more water, and increases dehydration. In response to this, most people replace this fluid loss with alcohol, which *further* acts to dehydrate the body. The solution, clearly, is to drink all the bottled water that you can on your flight (at least one to two glasses per hour).

Caveat emptor . . .

Due to the excess of physicians in most urban centers, some doctors have been carving out a profitable niche for themselves in the field of nutrition. Some of these doctors place undue emphasis on how complicated their subject is. These doctors sell not only their time and advice, but also a host of expensive food supplements, backed up with a battery of somewhat silly tests done on the urine, bits of hair, and so on. Often these are done as frequently as every week by the doctor's nurse.

Unsuspecting patients can become hooked on both the doctor and his or her supplements, at great expense, with little medically proven benefit. While such practitioners are few in number, they do command a loyal following. I would suggest that, before people invest their money in this type of treatment, they seek a second medical opinion to find out if it is truly necessary. Cases of severe dietary deficiency warranting such radical and expensive treatments are extremely rare on this continent.

In my own practice I find that most people do not need large doses of any one vitamin. I prefer them to get the bulk of their vitamin requirements from a proper, balanced diet. However, due to the depletion of zinc and vitamin C from the body under stress, and the apparent wisdom of taking vitamins C and E to help protect against cancer of the bowel, I usually recommend the daily use of a standard combination of these, such as a "stress" formulated tablet with zinc. Remember, if you have any of the many symptoms of vitamin deficiency, you need a diagnosis before treatment, so do consult your doctor.

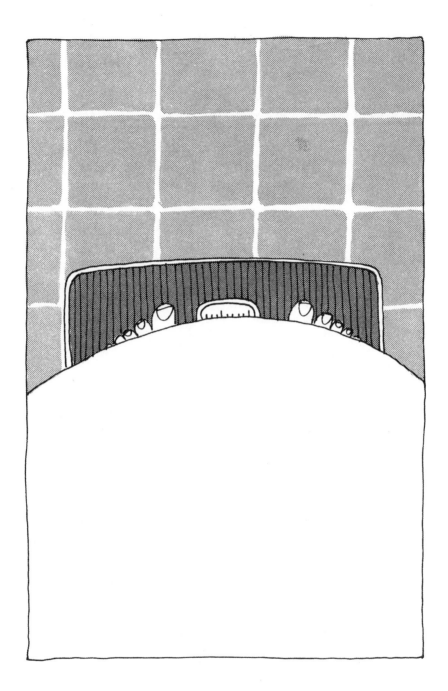

6.
Obesity
and Stress

As much as 40 percent of the population in North America is obese. By obesity, I mean anything more than 10 percent above your ideal body weight. Your "ideal" body weight is one-hundred pounds for the first five feet of height, and then five pounds per inch after that for women. For men, start at 115 pounds.

Thus a five-foot-six-inch woman should weigh approximately 130 pounds; a six-foot man should weigh 175 pounds. There may be wide fluctuations for build and frame, but you will know you are at your right weight if you feel your fittest and look your best in your bathing suit. Obesity is simply an imbalance in arithmetic. In order to be obese, you must take in more calories than you burn off. These excess calories are stored as fat. There are no ifs, ands, or buts; it is a simple, natural law.

One of the most common findings associated with obesity is denial. I had one patient come in and tell me that he just had "to look at food" to gain weight. All his coworkers at the factory could eat large lunches and stay thin. But he had only a small salad and soda water, and gained weight. He honestly believed that his problem was just bad luck and bad metabolism. After long and probing questioning, the patient admitted at last that he does get into the nut clusters by the boxful, and has a "leftovers" sandwich and chips before bedtime. His total average daily calorie count was in fact 3,500, while his output was only 1,500 calories. His weight was 262 pounds on a five-foot-nine-inch frame: 100 pounds overweight.

Obese people often deny that they are big eaters, and insist on remembering details of only the very modest lunches—the occasional half grapefruit and the few carrot slices that they consume during their days. It is important to remember that "binge eating," even if it occurs only once a month, must be added onto all the other calories that have been taken during the rest of the time period. That is, there is no point in eating a diet that has only eight-hundred calories per day from Monday to Friday if, on the weekends, you get into the nuts, chips, chocolates, or other favorite fattening foods, and put away five thousand calories in a few minutes. Denying that you ate these extra calories won't make them disappear.

The extra calories must be added to the average calorie intake of the other days of the week and, in fact, your body will be steadily adding them onto your total weight. Also remember, "picking" can add *thousands* of calories each day, without any conscious awareness of having eaten, particularly if you pick at foods low in fiber, which are not very filling to your stomach.

Obesity is never the problem. It is the *result* of your problem. The real cause of obesity is usually hidden beneath the surface. It will probably turn out to be one of the following:

1. Boredom.
2. Excess stress.
3. Lifestyle or peer pressure.
4. Poor self-image (unhappiness, depression).
5. All of the above.

1. Boredom can lead to obesity

Are you bored? Do you find yourself rearranging your spices according to the alphabet, or lining up your garden tools and kids' toys according to heights?

Ask yourself when you do most of your heavy eating, whether it is binges, picking, or heavy meals at certain times of the day or week. If boredom is a factor here, then make this the time of day that you do something to correct it. In other words, if you are bored in the evenings and tend to do most of your eating then, this would be an ideal time for you to engage in an enjoyable sport or other activity that you find stimulating and can do on a long-term basis. Pushups in the furnace room for a few days are not the answer. Spectator sports, while not exercise in themselves, are a useful diversion if they get you away from the fridge, but not if you end up overindulging in the hot dog and beer lineups instead.

If you are bored, examine your entire lifestyle, including asking yourself questions. Consider whether you are using your interests and skills to the best of your ability, trying to reach your potential. If not, you may find that you can make some changes, such as taking training courses to sharpen some of your skills. You may find stimulation either in the courses themselves or in subsequent part-time work.

Boredom can certainly be experienced by both sexes, and by all age groups. The solution to boredom in children and teens is usually quite obvious to parents, namely, that some structure or discipline has to be provided each day to give the child a sense of purpose. What we forget is that the same principles can apply to fighting boredom in adults and the elderly. Once boredom takes over, obesity becomes a willing companion. Certainly, if the highlight of your day is eating a pair of cupcakes and drinking a soda, you should reassess your priorities and organize yourself, to bring more happiness into your life from other sources.

Patients have told me that they choose to remain in what are essentially very monotonous jobs for the rest of their lives, as they could not afford to make a few dollars less and still keep up the lifestyle they have become accustomed to. However, if they calculate exactly how much money they need to live on, they may find they could get by on less, particularly if they could decrease the stress of having the wrong job. Moreover, by trading some money for greater happiness, they may increase their productivity in the long run.

If money still remains a goal, it can be sought in other ways, such as perhaps having a family member do some "moonlighting" at something the person enjoys and is good at.

2. Stress as a cause of overeating

Obesity is an abnormal physiological response to stress, as we have seen in Chapter 2. Your body tends to respond to stress by reducing its weight, burning up its stores of fat and sugar with an increased metabolism, triggered by increasing thyroid levels. However, some people have an overwhelming oral urge retained from childhood. Whenever stress strikes, they panic and shove something into their faces. My grandfather used to describe this as the "elbow-mouth" reflex: every time you bend your elbow, your mouth opens. In many cases the oral urge involves cigarettes or overeating, and often both. Oral oriented people are frequently seen chewing gum, sucking on mints, chewing their nails, and smoking—sometimes all at the same time.

Patients tell me that while they are eating as a response to stress, they know it is doing them harm. They know they will feel terrible about it a few minutes after they have finished eating, and often even *while* eating. But they "just can't" stop themselves. Most will admit to trying to eat quickly, as if to avoid being subconsciously "caught in the act," even by their own conscious selves. Speed, of course, only makes the stomach act as a trash compacter, and succeeds in packing in a much greater quantity of food before the stomach finally cries "full."

Food has a wonderful appeal to the senses of taste and smell, which can bring moments of pure ecstasy to the eater. When you think about it, if you have gone through a very stressful day, the guaranteed ecstasy of a favorite food does seem enticing. Such food can easily be incorporated into your balanced diet. However, under stress, the obese tend to eat beyond the point of satiety, to gratify the mouth even at the expense of straining the stomach.

3. Lifestyle and peer pressure as reasons for overeating

Lifestyle can be one of the most damaging reasons for overeating, as it usually begins in early childhood. The pressure actually starts with well-meaning parents who feel that a fat baby is a healthy one; that all the food on your plate must be finished; and that a reward for doing something well should be food, often a sweet. Children also imitate their parents in that, whenever company is invited, food must be made and served—usually food that is fattening. The association of food with all of these various activities and emotions is instilled at an early age, and can cause a lifetime of bad eating habits.

The peer pressure can begin when collections of overweight children get together and find they have common interests, which basically revolve around food. Often such children also share inactivity. They may sound active, and full of noise and energy, but they are actually burning off few calories in real exercise. The age at which obesity patterns usually commence in North American children is about six, or whenever they start school.

Ideally, every school day should start off with forty minutes of physical fitness training. A proper daily exercise routine at school should consist of fifteen minutes of stretching and warmup, followed by a twenty-minute period of high intensity exercise, and then a five-minute cooldown. The resulting improved concentration and attention span would easily make up for the forty minutes lost out of actual teaching time. It would also instill some lifelong daily habits that would virtually preclude the possibility of sloth in adult years.

Again, this brings up the importance of peer pressure. If all your friends are participating in sports, you will probably join them. But if they are all indulging in overeating and sedentary habits, you will probably feel pressure to join them in these inactivities.

Once you have exercised, and your whole body feels the glow of its muscle stiffness, you become aware of your body and less likely to absentmindedly overeat. As an added bonus, the endorphin generated by exercise acts as a natural appetite suppressant.

4. Poor self-image as a reason for overeating

Poor self-image is possibly the most significant and important reason for obesity. It is often immediately obvious from the way people dress and carry themselves—the nonverbal clues. I have had lengthy discussions with literally hundreds of people who would fit the mold of the "jovial, happy," fat person. Without exception, they all confess to putting this image forward as a façade, to hide their real problems, which often center around a poor self-image.

The joviality is actually a relatively good defense against being made a source of fun by others. Indeed, there is much to be said for retaining one's sense of humor in such conditions.

When you get up in the morning, you

should place yourself, and your body, at the very top of your list of things to do that day. Most people have a lengthy list of tasks to complete for others, but this usually doesn't include doing things for their own bodies. If you are suffering from a poor self-image, try a more positive approach. When you wake up in the morning and look into the bathroom mirror, try winking at yourself and saying, "Good morning, Beautiful." The fact that your first image each morning in the mirror may be a fright, with your silhouette being similar to that of a chicken hawk, should not deter you from the task at hand. Don't forget to go back and have another look in the mirror after you have finished getting dressed and ready for your day!

In spite of all the external factors, a poor self-image can still be overcome. There comes a time when excuses about your childhood wear a little thin. As an adult, every reasonable thing you wish to achieve is within your active control, through initiative, enterprise, and—most importantly—drive. If you set your targets too low, they will be easily achieved without developing these important qualities. If your self-image is good, then the sky is the limit, within the reality of your own skills and aptitudes.

The constant bombardment with media images emphasizing beauty, thinness, luxury, and wealth represents a sharp contrast for most people. Your own sense of self-worth sinks even lower if you are trying to compare yourself with the illusions of the silver screen. Your only question should be, am I the best that I am capable of being? My obese patients' answer is always the same, namely, that they are not even

"Whether you think you *can* or you *can't,* you're probably *right.*"

Henry Ford

If you think of yourself as being fat, you will be fat. If you think of yourself as being friendless and of no use to anyone, you can also fulfill those prophecies. The point is that negative images are self-destructive and self-fulfilling. There is no reason for anyone to have a poor self-image on a long-term basis, in spite of any excuse that might be offered. The excuse that I hear most often is that people have been told from early childhood by their parents that they should not strive for certain levels, as they cannot expect to ever be that competent or capable.

This seems to be more often true of women. It may account in part for there being more obese women than men (quite apart from hormonal considerations). In past generations, girls were usually treated as the second-class job prospects in the family. Most of the interesting career choices were suggested to the boys. Whether this was done deliberately or unconsciously, the result was the same. The list of "acceptable" jobs for girls was extremely limited. The reasoning was that the girls would be getting married and not needing a career. As adults, they may have found themselves to be fulfilling low expectations, as workers at the lower end of the job scale.

trying. They have a sense of resignation. They seem to have given up, and simply choose to think of themselves as "fat," with little potential for self-improvement.

It's your choice

Stress reduction can be realized by various means, including self-hypnosis techniques and positive thinking and imaging. I had one patient who gained a lot of weight after delivering her second child. She ultimately achieved success in losing weight from a five-year-old picture of herself looking slim in a bikini. She placed this picture on the front of her refrigerator. To the right of it was a short note: "It's *your* choice. You can choose *this* (with an arrow pointing to the picture), or *this* (with an arrow pointing in the direction of the refrigerator handle)." Her method was highly successful in creating a positive image to fight the thought of food. Undoubtedly you will develop your own favorite techniques that will work for you as well.

The "I just love eating" excuse

This excuse is one that is usually trotted out quite early by the obese person. We all love eating, and most people love good food. The problem occurs when the sense of proportion is warped, and the love of food assumes a much greater value than it should in comparison with other activities—or life itself. Even modest obesity (more than 10 percent above ideal body weight) can be harmful to your health. It is, therefore, quite obvious that, if you truly love eating, you will be able to eat for many more years if you pace yourself normally, rather than abusing the privilege.

7.
The Joy
of Stress
Food
Prescription:

Rx: Don't diet—eat normally

The very word *diet* has a punitive connotation;
you've *sinned* with overeating, and now you
have to go on a *diet*. The use of this one word
highlights all that is negative in your personality
(weak will power, lack of discipline, sneaky
closet eating followed by blatant denial, and so
on). Every time you use the word *diet*, you will
be reinforcing these negative images of yourself.
They thus become a self-fulfilled (and self-
filled) prophecy.

The first step in treating obesity is to correctly diagnose the cause, as we have just seen
in the last chapter. Once the real enemy has
been identified, you can harness your energy in
correcting it.

I approach obesity in a very positive way,
namely, emphasizing the positive attributes in

the patient's nature. The patient should take
stock of his or her good points—such as humor,
intelligence, and enjoyment of friends and family—and use creativity to put these to greater
use. I had one obese woman, for example, who
convinced her obese bridge group to switch to
an aerobics class, which none of them indi-
vidually would have had the nerve to attend.
They were all surprised to find that they had
not only never laughed so hard, but had a great
workout at the same time. As an added bonus,
they did not have plates of unneeded calories at
their fingertips; thus, they avoided absent-
minded consumption. The whole group felt
better about themselves, and were encouraged
to change their lifestyle for the better.

Rules for losing weight

1. Eat balanced meals, including all six food elements, for the rest of your life (see Chapter 5). It is no good plunging into a short-term diet emphasizing only some of these food elements.
2. Eat only from a plate. A small plate will give your meal the optical illusion of being piled high, rather than the image of sparsity that results when the same meal is spread out over a big plate.

3. Market the *right* snack foods to yourself; for example, have raw carrots sliced in a bowl of water at the front of the fridge, not in a bag in the drawer.
4. Sit down at the *table*. Eating while standing at the fridge or sink, or sitting in front of the TV, usually leads to absent-minded overeating. At the table, your mind is not distracted from the food.

5. Never eat without witnesses; in effect, don't eat behind everyone's back. Have you noticed how little most obese people eat when having dinner at someone else's house? Thin people are seen to eat large meals, but that's probably all they eat. They likely aren't sneak-snacking nearly as much as the obese.

6. Beware of any drinks with calories. Remember to allow for them in your total calorie budget. Calories from drinks are just as fattening as calories from foods.

7. Find and correct your *real* problem (see Chapter 6)—the problem that leads to your obesity.

8. Develop alternative rewards for yourself, other than eating, especially in response to stress.

9. Never shop for food when you are hungry. By the time you arrive home, your grocery bags may be nearly emptied by snacking.

10. Start *today.* Don't wait for an upcoming New Year's resolution, or for a sudden chest pain, to warn you of your impending ill health. The first serious warning that your body gives you could be your last breath. Consult your doctor for further advice.

Turning off the "fat-o-stat"

By way of illustration, when I am doing a week of vigorous downhill skiing, I can eat four thousand calories a day in such forms as a stack of pancakes for breakfast, chocolate bars and huge lunches on the hill, followed by big dinners and midnight snacks, and still not put on any weight because I burn it all off. If I ate like that back in my normal office routine, where I only burn off about fifteen hundred calories a day, I would soon be shaped like a giant avocado. It is important to have the ability to turn off one's "fat-o-stat" appropriately. This regulating mechanism seems to be broken in most people who are obese.

Learn that you can entertain without overeating

People commonly think they have to offer food along with their hospitality. Actually, you can go over to your neighbor's house for an afternoon or evening and have a nice visit without consuming hundreds of calories in cakes, nuts, and chips that neither of you would have had if you had not been together in the first place. One must learn to be able to have a conversation without using it as an excuse for having calories at the same time. If the calories are the only thing holding the conversation together, it obviously wasn't a very interesting conversation in the first place!

One of the reasons that most published diets fail over the long term is that they require you to have special, personal foods in the house—or else put the entire family on the diet. Such diets also do not allow for most restaurant meals, or special events such as weddings and dinner parties. One of the other problems with these diets is that they have you thinking about food all day long.

If you have success on a diet, of course you should stick with it, as long as it is balanced. However, after you have been dieting for six months or a year, if you find that your weight tends to come back up to where it was originally—or worse yet, even higher—then the whole process is obviously at fault. While you are on a diet, you are not learning anything new about yourself, your lifestyle habits, or your real problems. Once the diet is terminated, you are right back to your old habits of eating the wrong foods, carrying out the wrong activities, and getting ready to buy your next diet book.

"I can't help it; my slow metabolism makes me fat!" Wrong. You eat too much.

Develop a positive alternative when under stress, in order to compete with the enticing picture of food. If your choice under stress is between glorious food or nothing, quite obviously you are going to tend toward the former.

If, on the other hand, your choice is between food and *control*, with all the self-gratification and satisfaction that *control* implies, then suddenly you are faced with a proper choice and will be more likely to have the strength to turn down the food. If anything, the images of food will begin to pale in comparison to the images that you can associate with the confidence of gaining control over yourself. The picture of food can even be looked upon with some derision as a symbol of pure gluttony. The trick is to develop a positive image of your own that can be conjured up by all the same stresses that formerly conjured up just one picture, namely, that of food. This will require some thought, imagination, concentration, and practice. But it is indeed within your grasp.

Now that we have identified the various causes for overeating, let us consider what to do about it. A good first step is to be aware of the calories you already eat (see the appendix at the end of this book).

Most obese people will be shocked to find they consume several thousand calories per day—if they average in the total of all binges (even if they binge only once every few weeks). However, there are, of course, differences in the amounts of calories absorbed by different individuals' digestive tracts from a standard meal. There are also differences in calories burned off while asleep.

The Basic Metabolic Rate (BMR)—or calories that you burn off at rest all day, just to have your heart beating and lungs pumping—is about eight hundred calories. People blessed with a higher BMR may be able to burn off fifteen hundred calories per day without exercising, and seem to be able to eat anything and not get fat. Others may burn off only four hundred calories BMR, and have more of a problem losing weight. But whatever your BMR, you have to live with it. The only way to increase your metabolism is to increase your exercise each day.

Moderation Is the Key

When you are eating, you should certainly enjoy your food. Eat it slowly, and if you are preparing it, take care to make an attractive presentation. However, once you have finished eating, you should think no more about food. This is why my suggestion for counting calories is simply a guide for the first few weeks, and should not become an obsession. As long as your weight is on a downward trend of at least a pound per week, you need never again refer to the number of calories. However, if you find that you have reached a plateau for more than two weeks, or that your weight is creeping back up, then it becomes imperative to find out what the problem is.

At such a time, it would be appropriate to go back to the basics and count your calorie intake. It is very important for you to still have some of your favorite foods. For example, if you are big on ice cream sundaes, which you know you will never find on any diet sheet, then I would suggest you still have one on occasion. Of course, this should be a small-sized version, and should be taken as a reward, preferably when everybody else is having the same thing. And no more often than once a week! Thereafter, if you find yourself watching others eating ice cream—or worse yet, if you have to serve it to other members of the family—you will not feel so hard done by.

Moderation is a very important concept. All you need to learn is *normality* in eating habits, and in lifestyle habits. Food should be one of your enjoyments, but not your only one. Your time is too valuable to waste on just this aspect of your life.

Some Guidelines for Exercising

It is important, when looking at the calorie burn-off guide, to try and pick an activity that is both fun and practical for you. I do not advise obese people to jog on pavement, as this is just asking for trouble with hips, knees, arches, and the spine. Riding a bicycle, however, is quite safe, since the feet do not touch the ground. Swimming is also recommended, as gravity is neatly avoided. Even a hippopotamus can run gracefully under water!

Once involved in exercise, take the same precautions a full-time athlete would take, including warmup and cooldown stretching exercises. Strong stomach muscles are required for such routine matters as standing upright, avoiding backache from "sway-back," preventing constipation, and for virtually every sport. (See Chapter 5.) However, *no* sport (except a few such as gymnastics and body building) does much to build strong stomach muscles. Thus, even marathoners, ski racers, bicyclists, and swimmers need to include daily stomach exercises in their routines.

Beware of the fast

After months, years, or even decades of losing the daily battle with the refrigerator, most obese people get frustrated and angry at themselves. They want to lose weight, but are in an unrealistic and desperate hurry, and are often vulnerable to weight-loss schemes promising overnight results. The ultimate method would appear to be to *fast;* the very word seems to impart a certain impression of speed to the process.

But if we pause here and reflect on the arithmetic, this is just not possible. To lose one pound, you must have an energy shortfall of 3,500 calories; that is, 500 calories per day of decreased food intake or increased exercise expenditure. (See Appendix C.) This equals one pound of weight loss per week. This rate of loss is not as useless as it at first seems—it means you would lose fifty-two pounds in a year, which is probably better than you did last year.

But if you find that you are eating an extra one thousand or two thousand calories above your daily requirements, then you will be able to lose weight in multiples of this rate. That is, if you can spare one thousand calories per day from your intake, you will lose two pounds per week; two thousand calories per day will mean a four-pound per week loss, and so on.

In the initial week of any diet, an encouraging extra weight loss is seen in the form of fluid loss. This is because the extra calories that are missing were usually consumed with salt (either in the food, or added at the table). When the salt load is moderated, fluid will be lost (see page 135).

Figure 7.1

Calories used in various activities (per hour)*

	130 LBS. BODY WEIGHT	150 LBS. BODY WEIGHT	250 LBS. BODY WEIGHT
Aerobic dancing	395	490	540
Baseball	250	310	340
Basketball	670	830	910
Bicycling—10 mph	370	460	505
Bowling	240	300	325
Chess	80	100	110
Digging	445	555	610
Eating	80	100	110
Gardening	345	430	470
Housework—general	180	225	235
Lawn mowing—power	225	280	295
Mountain climbing	535	665	730
Rowing—2 mph	270	335	365
Shopping	150	185	205
Sleeping	60	75	80
Tennis	380	470	520
Walking—3 mph	270	336	366
Washing a car	205	255	280
Yoga	205	255	280

*The same rates apply to fractions of an hour's exercise. For example, one-half hour of bowling for a 150-pound person will burn off 150 calories.

Figure 7.2

The calorie content of some favorite foods

Apple	75
Apple pie	300
Apple pie with ice cream	450
Bacon, 3 slices	120
Banana	100
Beans, green fresh	10
Beer	150
Bread, one slice	60
Butter, one pat	50
Carrots, one-half cup	25
Cashews, one oz.	150
Cheese, one oz.	100
Chicken fried, one serving	300
Coffee or tea, black	0
Cookies, 2 small plain	100
Eclair	275
Grapefruit, one-half	30
Halibut, average serving	100
Ham, baked one slice	350
Hamburger, 4 oz.	400
Honey, one tablespoon	65
Lettuce, one-quarter head	10
Martini	125
Milk, 8 oz. whole	170
Orange juice, 4 oz.	55
Peanuts, 10	100
Pork chop, one medium	150
Potato, French fries, 30 sticks	465
Potato, boiled, one medium	50
Rib steak, average serving	320
Salad dressing, one tablespoon	100
Salmon, one serving	250

Sugar, one teaspoon 18
Tomato soup, one cup 100
Wine, glass 100

The above list serves to show that your daily calorie intake can be anything that you wish it to be. Avoid high calorie foods, and you are well on the way to success. (For a more extensive calorie listing, see Appendix C at the back of this book.)

It is a shock to find that the number of calories burned off by scrubbing the kitchen floor for an hour (a guaranteed backache) doesn't even equal the number found in a piece of apple pie. This may not seem fair, but it is a fact of life. In order to "earn," or "deserve," a piece of pie and ice cream, you would have to go bicycling for an hour. It is not hard to see how food intake can quite readily get ahead of calorie expenditure. Calories can come in very compact forms. For example, one pound of cashews has about 2,400 calories; ten peanuts have 100 calories (and no one eats just ten—be honest!). Just three glasses of pop could add 300 calories without diminishing your appetite.

The "Eat Normally" Balance Sheet

"Your Daily Reckoning"

1. Weigh yourself initially, and again at the same time of day at the end of each week. Do *not* weigh yourself more often. (Otherwise the three to four pounds of daily fluid

fluctuation in the body will lead to false confidence or despair.) It may be best to arrange to have the weighing done at your doctor's office. You may not need to see the doctor each time. I have my secretary record the weekly weights of my obese patients, and I see them only if they gain weight. This partial reinforcement works very well.

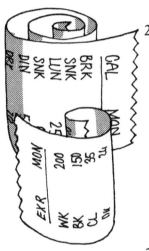

2. Enter the daily calorie count of *everything* that you put into your mouth, including drinks, gum, candy, and so on. Right away, this will make you less likely to have absent-minded snacks. Record your daily calorie count for as many days as it takes you to get into a normal eating routine. Keep track of your daily *average;* for example, you may eat more on weekends than mid-week. If you are good, developing a normal routine may take only a few weeks initially, and can be restarted whenever you are shocked by a weight gain. You should not need to dwell on the numbers of calories forever.

3. Enter the number of minutes of active exercise each day. This will serve two purposes: it will allow you to roughly calculate the calories burned off, and it will remind you to do some exercise before you call it a day. Remember to consult your doctor to help you choose a level and type of exercise that is safe for your overall condition.

4. Show your written records to your doctor—he or she will be able to see where your problems lie, especially if you fail to lose weight.

The fact that insurance companies have recently enlarged the allowable weights for each height by a few pounds should not be seen as any kind of green light for obesity. The death statistics for obesity are still disastrous. In the long run, they average one death per patient.

Get out your calculators!

FIRST WEEK:	TOTAL CALORIES CONSUMED (SEE FIGURE 7.2 OR APPENDIX C)		TOTAL CALORIES BURNED OFF (SEE FIGURE 7.1)
Day 1		cal.	cal.
Day 2		cal.	cal.
Day 3		cal.	cal.
Day 4		cal.	cal.
Day 5		cal.	cal.
Day 6		cal.	cal.
Day 7		cal.	cal.

Sub-total   cal.   Sub-total   cal.

÷ 7 =   Calorie intake per day   ÷ 7 =   Calorie burn-off per day

CALORIE INTAKE   **–**   **=**

Average calories consumed per day   Average calories burned off per day   Average net calories intake per day

WEIGHT CHANGE   **–**   **=**

Starting weight on Day 1   Weight after first week   Weight change in one week

(For additional sheets see Appendix C)

The only two numbers you need to know are: the net average daily calorie intake, and your weight change at the end of each week.

If your weight is declining at a rate of at least one pound per week, then you can leave your net calorie intake as it is. If not, then you have just two options: Reduce calories taken in, or increase calories burned off. There are a number of additional techniques that can help you lose weight. These include hypnosis, as well as acupuncture. While it is beyond the scope of this book to deal with each of these in detail, both have definite merit. I have used acupuncture very successfully on some of my own patients and have also sent others to a hypnotist with good results.

Acupuncture techniques work best for people who tend to suffer "withdrawal" when they change their eating habits. As we have seen, acupuncture produces *endorphin* from the hypothalamus. This tends to act in exactly the same ways as morphine does from outside the body, which may explain why morphine addicts do not tend to be fat. Endorphin tends to give a sense of well being and provides an alternative to seeking gratification from food. It has been shown to be a useful treatment for withdrawal in morphine addicts, as the endorphin occupies the same receptor sites in the brain. Acupuncture has also been found to be useful in treating people experiencing withdrawal from smoking, alcohol, or overeating. However, there are a number of other psychological triggers (besides withdrawal) that make people eat; for example, the Pavlovian ringing of the lunch bell. These are best dealt with through other techniques such as hypnosis. Of course, the best method of all is to be able to help yourself according to the above guidelines. If you need additional support, consult your doctor for help or for referral. Unqualified hypnotists and lay acupuncturists can be detrimental to your health.

Diet pills used to work very well, as they used to be amphetamines, or "speed." A whole generation of fat people were commonly given these "uppers," and the side effects were dreadful. After a week of vacuuming the ceiling, dusting the roof of the house, and forgetting to sleep or eat, the obese patient would certainly lose a few pounds. However, there were serious risks of heart attack and other problems, and basically *nothing* was learned. The patient soon reverted to the same old habits, and up went the weight.

The new diet pills are a weak version of their predecessors and are essentially useless (unless taken with very little daily food). Diet pill users often get caught needing "downers" or tranquilizers to sleep, thus even further weakening their resistance to stress (see Chapter 3).

Real help for obesity does not come in pill form!

Conclusion

When you are reducing, you should *organize* your life so that you are enjoying yourself, and not thinking about food for any more time than it takes you to prepare and eat your meals. If you are thinking about food any more often than this, then you have not learned much, and are likely to go right back to the same old patterns of obesity.

Remember that you should fight obesity not simply for the sake of aesthetics. This is a point on which the minority groups for the preservation of fat people's rights are quite at fault. I don't feel any organization should advocate people's rights to commit suicide with a knife, fork, and several tons of groceries. Such organizations merely provide more peer pressure on obese people to stay fat.

What we are dealing with here is a definite detriment to your health. Obesity will shorten both the span and enjoyment of your life. If you are obese, you are putting your heart, lungs, pancreas, joints, spine—in fact your entire body—at risk. If you correct this, you will live longer.

More importantly, you will be able to function in a more youthful way. For example, maybe you'll still be around—and fit enough—to exercise with your grandchildren, and with their children. It's certainly something to aim at! It's very selfish to deny your heirs the pleasure of your company. Why cheat them out of knowing you just for the sake of a few absent-minded binges? And one last benefit—if you live more years, you will be able to eat more food in your total lifetime, so *pace* yourself!

8.
Stress and Your Heart

*Heart disease—
inevitable or preventable?*

Heart disease is one of the most complex and hotly debated subjects in the medical profession. Much is still unknown. However, some factors have been clearly identified as risks. Most are within your control.

1. Diabetes mellitus.

Also known as *sugar diabetes*. Diabetes can be associated with heart attacks. This disease has also been called *premature aging*. Proper diagnosis and cooperation between patient and doctor are extremely important.

2. Hypertension.

Usually silent, with no symptoms at all, but can be a big cause of hardening of the arteries and coronary attacks. In between visits, your doctor may suggest you record your blood pressure readings at home, in order to accurately pick up the highs and lows. Early detection, frequent checks with your doctor, and often drug therapy can eliminate most of the risks of high blood pressure.

3. Hereditary hypercholesterolemia.

In severe cases of this, few males in a given family will reach age forty without having a heart attack. Although the condition is fortunately quite rare, it is always best to check with your family doctor for your serum cholesterol levels. It is even more important if the male members of your family tended to have early heart attacks. I have seen some families in which the males do not live longer than forty-one or forty-two years because of this condition, with cholesterol deposits blocking coronary arteries. Early diagnosis is important. The best results are obtained if the diagnosis is made before age ten, and appropriate cholesterol reducing measures are taken. It is in such cases that it can be extremely important to avoid eating cholesterol. (See Chapter 5.)

4. Hyperthyroidism.

Now fortunately quite rare.

5. Smoking.

Cigarettes are known to cause instant constriction of the blood vessels in the coronary arteries. The many ways in which this outrageous habit harms your heart and the rest of your body are discussed more fully in Chapter 3.

6. Sloth.

Regular exercise doesn't guarantee protection from heart disease, but evidence suggests it certainly helps. Note that "intermittent sloth" can be terribly bad for you; sudden sprints when out of shape, such as are required in racquet sports, baseball, jogging, and so on can be fatal.

Consult your doctor and a qualified exercise professional for assistance.

7. *Type A behavior.*

This will be discussed in the following pages.

> ### *The cholesterol controversy: more food for thought*
>
> Cholesterol, currently the subject of controversy, has already been discussed in Chapter 5. A high cholesterol intake doesn't necessarily increase the risk of heart disease. One frequently cited example is the study of Boston Irishmen versus their brothers in Ireland. The latter were eating a great deal of cholesterol, whereas the former were eating foods low in cholesterol. Their respective rates of heart disease were not at all what one might have expected; the Boston brothers had the higher rate of heart attacks.
>
> Other groups, such as Navaho Indians and the Masai people of Africa, also eat high cholesterol diets and have very little coronary heart disease. Americans have three times the amount of coronary heart disease today that they had in 1910, but still eat a similar amount of cholesterol. It is thus obvious that there are more factors at play than simple dietary intake, and these are being studied intensively. Other factors that probably play a part include the amount of fiber in the diet; Type A behavior; exercise; and most importantly, resistance to stress (see Chapters 3 and 4).

Type A behavior: Self-induced stress

An understanding of Type A behavior, first described by Dr. Meyer Friedman in his book *Type A Behavior and Your Heart,* has provided a great deal of insight into the most common link among heart attack patients. Quite often, such patients have an "action-emotion" complex. This basically consists of "hurry sickness." Such people are constantly watching the clock, and fighting it every step of the way. They have an excessive competitive drive, with easily aroused hostility.

The Type A person is aggressive, in a chronic struggle to achieve more in less time, even at the expense of offending others. He or she can be very hostile if threatened. Although such a person may seem like a "jerk" in some ways, it is interesting to note that more often than not, his or her activities are socially praised, and rewarded with material goods.

Type A behavior is seen in up to half of all males, and in an increasing number of females in the work force. When given a simple test, such as subtracting 13's from 1,000 in a given time period, Type A people perform as well as Type B, who have all the opposite traits. The difference is that the Type A's treat the test as an emergency. They respond with forty times the amount of cortisol secreted into the bloodstream, three times the amount of blood flow to the muscles, and four times as much adrenalin surging through the blood vessels. As seen in Chapter 2, this means that all the stress responses are activated, including increased

cholesterol in the blood, racing of the heartbeat, and so on.

Many successful companies now have stress
programs, but usually just for executives. However, even more stress often comes to those in
middle management (lots of responsibility, but
very little control). Companies should be concentrating on extending their stress reduction
programs to all those who need it. The payback
in reducing sick and absentee time and increasing productivity is incredible. For every dollar
invested in preventive medicine, the return can
be as much as five dollars.

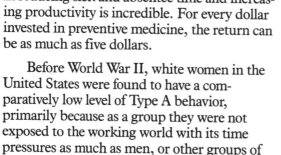

Before World War II, white women in the
United States were found to have a com-
paratively low level of Type A behavior,
primarily because as a group they were not
exposed to the working world with its time
pressures as much as men, or other groups of
women. However, this is certainly changing
with the modern economic facts of life.

In a ten-year study, Type A personalities
were *three times* as likely to have coronary heart
diseases. In predicting who was going to have a
heart attack, Type A behavior was found to be
more important than other factors, including
family history, serum cholesterol levels, and
smoking.

In order to learn about the effects of Type A
behavior on health, studies were done on rats.
Specimens had specific damage done to the
brain (the hypothalamus), which caused them
to develop Type A behavior. These rats were
shown to tolerate Type B rats in the same cage,
because of the lack of fear of competition. However, when a Type A rat from this group was
placed in a cage with another Type A rat, the

two of them fought to the death. A similar effect may be seen with two Type A humans. Often this is evident in a fiercely competitive form of one-upmanship between neighbors, or peers at work. It can also be a disastrous combination in a marriage, unless resolved.

As part of the overall reflex responses to stress seen in the "alarm phase" in Type A rats (see Figure 2.3), it was noted that cholesterol levels in the blood could be dramatically increased irrespective of the amount of dietary cholesterol consumed. The cholesterol question is discussed more fully on pages 114-118.

*O*ne interesting sidelight is that the key link between Type A behavior and heart disease was first noted not by researchers, but by Dr. Friedman's upholsterer. The upholsterer came into the doctor's cardiology office to recover the chairs, and asked what kind of patients the doctor had. He had noted that the fabric on the chairs was worn out only across the front edges. No one had been sitting back and relaxing in those chairs. "On the edge of the seat" behavior is, of course, typical of Type A individuals.

Some Type A characteristics

Hurry sickness.

Sets too many deadlines; not adaptable or
creative; relies on forms or creative ideas developed when he or she was more efficient. Not
very good at attacking new problems, due to
inflexibility. (Needs to be more like the Type
B—to ponder, and use creativity.)

Numbers.

Begins with childhood, the fun of acquisition,
and of counting one's things, such as marbles,
baseball cards, girlfriends. Maturity should
moderate this, but such is often not the case.

Score keeping.

Done to soothe insecurity. Doesn't enjoy a golf
game for the fine scenery and fresh air, but is
intently concentrating on the score every step of
the way. Heaven help Type A's if they get interested in gambling!

ME	THEM
﹘﹘	﹘﹘
﹘﹘	﹘﹘
﹘﹘	l
ll	

Insecurity.

Seeks approval from his or her boss more than
from peers. A Type A person couldn't be just a
regular scientist, for instance. He or she would
aspire to be a superstar, by publishing large
numbers of papers, and so on.

Hostility and aggression.

The urge to compete: may have a sense of
humor, but generally only to laugh at others
rather than at himself or herself.

How to tell Type A from Type B behavior

Type A

1. Sharp aggressive style of speech; the end of the sentence is faster.
2. Easily bored; tunes out, only pretending to listen.
3. Always eats, talks, and walks quickly.
4. Impatient with others who dawdle; for example, saying "yes, yes" to speed up someone else's speech, or worse yet, finishing their sentences for them.
5. Polyphasic; for example, eating, shaving, and reading all at the same time. (Needs to take care to avoid getting dressed and showered simultaneously.)
6. Selfish. Interested only in conversation about things that relate to him or her; tries to steer conversation his or her way, or tunes out. (After spending a considerable time talking about himself on a TV talk show, a Type A author turned to the host of the program and said, "Well, enough of all this talk about me; let's talk about you. Tell me, what did *you* think about my book?")
7. Feels guilty when relaxing.
8. Not observant. Can't remember details of rooms, and so on. Most likely to be the one to lose keys, sunglasses, pen.
9. Aims for things worth *having*, not things worth *being*.
10. Very challenged by another Type A individual. Sparks can fly. This is particularly bad if two Type A's are married to each other.

11. Physical signs: very assertive, tense, leans forward, shoulder blades seldom touch the chair (or even the rib cage for that matter).
12. Believes success comes from doing things faster; thus keeps up a very fast pace. Believes that when you are skating on thin ice, the only thing you have going for you is *speed.*
13. Measures success mainly by numbers; for example, more interested in number of goals scored than with pleasure of playing a game.

Type B

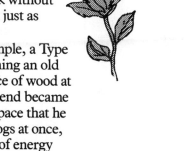

1. Not characterized by the above traits.
2. Seldom feels any time urgency, but can be just as ambitious.
3. Very easygoing; not hostile.
4. Plays a game for fun, not just to win.
5. Can relax without guilt and work without agitation; in the long run can get just as much work done as a Type A.
6. Is often more efficient. For example, a Type A friend of mine was once watching an old woodcutter neatly stack one piece of wood at a time against his garage. My friend became so agitated at the apparent slow pace that he rushed outside, picked up five logs at once, and with a frenetic expenditure of energy started his own stack of wood. After twenty minutes he collapsed, exhausted, back aching, with his pile of wood in a mess, and only a fraction as large as the old man's. Type B's, it seems, often win because of their steadiness and their economy of movement. (Perhaps this is what the old "Hare and Tortoise" fable was trying to tell us.)

Type A behavior and "the third wave"

In connection with Type A behavior, it is interesting to note Alvin Toffler's book *The Third Wave*. According to Toffler, the First Wave of civilization was agricultural, with hand-to-mouth subsistence, and people living wherever there was arable land. The Second Wave was born with the Industrial Revolution, during which the importance of mass production at centralized urban factories was emphasized. Also, at this time, working against the time clock came into being, with the advent of assembly lines and deadlines. With the spirit of free market competition developed the continual race to do more, thus leading to a great increase in Type A behavior.

Individuals who succeeded in acquiring *things* were extolled. Even in the early 1800s America was noted to be Type A both at work and at home, with a willingness to constantly uproot families in order to upgrade job postings. On holidays, Americans used to have the "ugly American" reputation (now no longer monopolized by any one nationality). Type A vacation trips are overly ambitious. Type A holidayers try to visit too many cities, countries, or relatives within a short time frame. They try to impress their peers by numbers, whether it be how many countries they visited while in Europe, how many miles per day they were able to drive without stopping, or how fast they could go.

With the diminishing importance of the old class system, life following the Industrial Revolution was, to a great extent, like a land rush or gold rush, in which everyone could make a fortune if only he or she ran fast enough.

This Second Wave behavior has certainly brought North Americans up to the highest standard of living in the world, leaving First Wave countries in the dust (literally).

However, we are now into what is known as the Third Wave, or the Technological Revolution. People no longer have to go to central factories to earn a living. The possibilities exist for the rebirth of small "cottage" industries; for example, a computer programmer could easily work at home. His or her work can be transmitted via satellite to a central computer bank.

New stresses are brought to bear in this Third Wave. But there is definitely hope that the mass urbanization of the last two centuries, during which large numbers of people moved to cities, could be reversed. If this happens people will regain some control over their lives—an element that is often lacking in overcrowded areas.

With the advent of the Industrial Revolution, and the increase of Type A behavior, the stressors that one faced in life went from simple to very complex. Instead of being threatened by the attack of a wild animal, for instance, people were threatened by complex stressors such as insidious noise pollution and time pressures. With our current position in the Third Wave, stressors are now likely to become even better disguised. Thus it is more important than ever to maintain your body in its best possible condition, and develop correct skills and choices to assist you in your defense against stress.

The excessive competition characterizing

Type A behavior was often not present in the rural life of yore; subsistence was enough. However, in modern times it seems that each generation of children expects to continue to compete. This includes bettering its lifestyle as compared to that of its parents. Although this is not a hereditary feature, it is certainly one that is fostered by Type A parents, who put excessive emphasis on the acquisition of *things*.

The only way to please a typical Type A parent is for a child to achieve higher grades, clock a faster time in a race, or beat more people in competition. In other words, "Winning is everything" seems to be the credo. But just as those who suffer from the "bigger boat" syndrome are doomed to forever being beaten by one-upmanship, children can eventually become disillusioned with this approach to life, and set their own courses. In my own practice I find that the biggest rifts between teenagers and parents occur in Type A families.

"Rich man, poor man ... "

The sense of excessive competition may be worst among the middle classes, who always seem to have to "prove themselves." The rich may have a potential advantage, in financial security. What the wealthy view as bad mannered *"nouveaux riches"* behavior is often just the Type A behavior pattern. In England, the "old rich" are naturally Type B in their behavior, having never been involved personally in the race against the time clock.

The wealthy are never in the same "land rush" race as the rest of the population, mainly because they already own all the land. Most chief executive officers of corporations are Type

B personalities (including the president of the United States, Ronald Reagan), but the good ones are smart enough to hire Type A employees, to help their companies succeed. The trick is to keep the Type A person in close check, so that he or she remains in the position of peak stress performance. (See chart on page xx.)

*T*here are, of course, many disadvantages to wealth. The wealthy can suffer from a lack of initiative or incentive to work hard. Other difficulties may include boredom, problems in finding good help, polo injuries, having to learn French so they can have arguments in front of the servants, and sore backs because the rear seats of their chauffeur-driven cars don't recline.

Tips to changing from Type A to Type B behavior

1. Recognize you probably won't suffer financially by being Type B. Do not confuse ambition or drive with being Type A only. Any success you have already achieved is likely in *spite* of your Type A behavior. Type B people can still get the job done well. They have just as much ambition, but don't seem to panic while they achieve their goals.

2. Learn to laugh, not just at others, but at yourself. Most Type A humor is made up of a litany of jokes and anecdotes at the expense of others.

3. Expand your horizons with an alternate activity, preferably something that does not involve racing against the stopwatch. If you have your own library at home, try reading the books in it—rather than just acquiring them by the linear yard. If you buy a bicycle, do *not* buy a computerized speedometer and mileage recorder; just *enjoy* your bike rides.

4. Get organized. For your heart's sake, learn to let others take over the less important tasks—things that can be delegated. Even though you *can* do something doesn't mean that you *should* do it. Think about what jobs could be better left to someone else, to allow you to get on with more important tasks. This applies to your work, and even more so to your home life. Hiring a student to do some of the gardening could give you peace of mind, plus more quality time with your family.

5. Avoid other Type A's when possible. If you can't avoid them; for example, if you are married to one, then shut up. Try to avoid your tendency to constantly compete. Aim more at *complementing* and *helping* your spouse, rather than *outdoing* him or her.
6. Aim for things worth *being*, not worth *having*.
7. Try exercises that force you to slow down; for example, if you jump an amber light, circle the block; go back and do it properly. Try conversing with a slow thinker and not interrupting or finishing sentences for him or her. If you are getting steamed under the collar in a slow bank line, let a couple of people go by—it won't kill you!
8. Try driving for half an hour behind anyone wearing a hat, without honking or passing.
9. Try watching anyone do *anything* in the post office without barking at them to speed up.
10. Try watching an entire PBS talk show on social issues and suburban administration in the 1980s without changing channels.
11. Try sitting quietly through a PTA meeting on the importance of Freudian psychological analysis for all grade one students.
12. Try attending any volunteer committee meeting and *not speaking*.

We all face a large daily dose of stress from our surroundings; what you *don't* need is *self-induced* stress on top of this background. Therefore, do everything in your power to eradicate Type A behavior from your life

Self-induced stress: Diary of a Type A day

PLANNED DAY	**ACTUAL DAY**
7:05 Rise and shine; organize clothes.	Slept through alarm clock; wore brown shoes with blue suit.
8:00 Meet Glenn for one hour re: ad campaign.	Caught in rush hour traffic; arrived twenty minutes late.
9:30 Meet Jim across town re: year end.	False start—had to turn around to go back for briefcase at Glenn's. Then got stuck behind some slow *imbecile* in the fast lane . . . made me late.
10:00 Back to office for phone calls for one hour. Make sixteen urgent callbacks left from yesterday.	First two phone calls unearthed surprise, time-consuming problems. Had to postpone fourteen important callbacks until tomorrow, or maybe the next day.

11:05 Pick up VIPs at airport. Don't be late!	Passed every car on the road to get there on time. Left the car illegally parked. VIPs' plane was late.
11:30 Have VIPs back for boardroom meeting. Look sharp!	Paced in airport for half an hour waiting for VIPs. Then spent forty minutes getting car out of the pound. Phoned office to advise of delay. Picked up eight more urgent messages.
12:00 Lunch and tennis doubles with important account. Us against two members of a competing firm.	Road construction! Arrived late, missed lunch. Started set by serving up four consecutive double faults. Threw racquet against back wall, picked up balls, and walked off . . .

Obviously, one of the problems this person has is under-estimating the amount of time required to carry out planned activities. Properly used, a time and priority management system can be a most valuable stress aid. It should have times listed for all 168 hours in each week and be used *especially* for your spare time, not only work appointments. The discipline involved in using such a system pays enormous dividends in efficiency, quality of time, sense of accomplishment (as tasks are ticked off), improved self-image, and less troubled sleep due to avoidance of unresolved or omitted details.

Conclusion

Do not allow Type A behavior to narrow your coronary arteries, undermine your family life, waste your profits, and shorten your time on earth. Pause, reflect, and reset your priorities.

It is just as simple to join the (Type) "B Team." You must first recognize that your ambitions, goals, and lifestyle can be *better* achieved with the Type B personality, and that success does not depend on the frenetic nervous energy of the Type A personality. As a bonus, changing to Type B behavior will give you strength instead of weakness in the *health, job, financial,* and *personal* quadrants of your life. As we will see in the next chapter, these are the four areas to consider in predicting a long, healthy, and prosperous life. Read on.

■

9.
The
"Secrets"
of Long Life
and Prosperity

I have interviewed hundreds of healthy people born in the last century, and asked their secrets for a long, prosperous life. The answers were diverse, but a pattern emerged.

Those who lived *well* into their tenth decade tended to be rated as a *"success"* in all four quadrants of their lives, as seen in this chart:

Figure 9.1

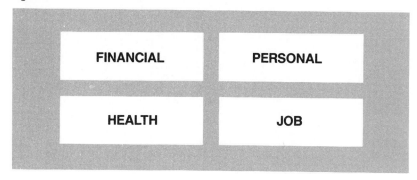

FINANCIAL   PERSONAL

HEALTH   JOB

Success means striving toward excellence in *all four* quadrants. Failure to address *any* of these quadrants will predictably shorten your life and decrease productivity in the workplace.

1. Financial Quadrant.

Success means having saleable job skills, adequate money for your goals, and security in case of ill health, recession, or loss of job. It need *not* involve having millions, but simply living within one's budget.

2. Personal Quadrant.

Success here means a stable base of true friends (not necessarily large numbers) and family; in particular, a happy marriage or similar relationship.

3. Health Quadrant.

Success means being in sound health (both mental and physical) confirmed by your doctor's opinion, not just your own. Correct choices of lifestyle and resistance to stress (see Chapter 4) must be made.

4. Job *(or, if still a student, Education)* Quadrant.

Success here means performing efficiently, with integrity, and earning the respect of peers.

Success: The key to longevity

As indicated in Figure 9.1, success may be
divided into four equal compartments. In order
to achieve your maximum enjoyment and span
of life, you should address them all. Success in
only one out of the four actually constitutes
failure, even if that success is in the financial
field or job-education field; for example, the
research genius or A student.

You should strive toward excellence in all
four quadrants. This requires care and attention being paid to each. Following are some
true-to-life examples of successes in just one or
two quadrants. Note that S indicates success;
F indicates failure. Add up the Fs for your
total. Even one F equals net failure, and predictable decline of both the quantity and
quality of life.

Howard Hughes in His Later Years

REPORT CARD

Financial Quadrant—S.

Storybook success; money beyond anyone's dreams.

Personal Quadrant—F.

He ended up lonely, with no stable base at home. He had to hire people to love him and care for him.

Health Quadrant—F.

His health was terrible. Physically he was wasted, shriveled, frail, and so weak that he needed to be carried everywhere. Mentally, it would be a fair opinion to say that in his later life certainly the spots had come off his dice. His obsession with gaining complete privacy, even from germs, is only one confirmation of this.

Job Quadrant—F.

Enjoyed little admiration from his peers, other than a grudging respect for his success in the financial quadrant. He conducted his business in a rather ruthless manner, and did not bother about making lasting friendships along the way.

Final Score—3 Fs.

One out of four successes equals a net failure and a predictable decrease in the quality and quantity of life.

Marilyn Monroe in Her Last Years

REPORT CARD

Financial Quadrant—S.

Personal Quadrant—F.

Life of tragedy; search for stability and love.

Health Quadrant—F.

Health includes *mental* well-being as well as physical. Disastrous in Monroe's case; addicted to drugs; mentally unstable.

Job Quadrant—S.

Well respected by peers and public; in fact, a tremendous success.

Final Score—2 Fs.

Two out of four quadrants successful; net result still a predictably decreased quality and quantity of life.

"Joe Family Man"

Profile

Great with his young kids, but not an achiever. After his plant closed, he gave up looking for work and chose to stay home and collect welfare. Even the loving spouse is beginning to get a little cheesed at him for being around so much, and at the financial hardships that this entails. After a few half-hearted attempts at applying for work, boredom sets in. Self-image and esteem in the eyes of the family also suffer.

REPORT CARD

Financial Quadrant—F.

Personal Quadrant—S.

A great guy; popular with the kids and neighbors; a loving and warm person.

Health Quadrant—F.

The lack of mental stimulation and the *absence* of stress from the workplace begin to dull Joe's intellect. His efficiency is down. Now it takes him almost all day just to finish reading the TV Guide. He starts to gain weight, smoke cigarettes, drink more alcohol, and get less exercise than he used to.

Job Quadrant—F.

What job?

Final Score—3 Fs.

Net failure and likely shortened marriage expectancy and a probable decrease in the quality and quantity of life.

"Joe Fist"

Profile

Five hours a day pumping weights and amino acids. Although bodybuilding is an outstanding exercise, he carries it to excess, and has become an "exercisaholic." Posing in front of mirrors constitutes most of his social life. A great physical specimen, but at the expense of his working and social life.

REPORT CARD

Financial Quadrant—F.

Does not have the time to work overtime, or to put forth extra effort in the evenings to try and get ahead in his career. He works only hard enough to make ends meet.

Personal Quadrant—S.

Self-confident and attractive to others.

Health Quadrant—S.

The very peak of health; exercise tolerance excellent; good low heart rate; has three square bowel movements per day. However, it is a fact that body builders as a group do not hold any longevity records in spite of their remarkable conditioning.

Job Quadrant—F.

Joe is an underachiever here, doing rather menial and boring work, because he is not prepared to spend the extra time to excel or get training that will put him into a job that he enjoys. Most careers and social lives would not leave time for his obsessive five hours of weight training per day.

Final Score—2 Fs.

Failure, with predictable decrease in quality and, ultimately, quantity of life.

"Wendy Workaholic"

Profile

As a student, she was intense. She worked hard on her studies, but spent little time on the "frivolities" of social functions, sports, or developing personal relationships with her peers. Has worked her way up to a responsible position. The problem is, she's "hooked" on her work. She's interested in very little else. She can't even tear herself away for a short holiday. If she does, she's miserable until she gets back to the office.

REPORT CARD

Financial Quadrant—S.

Though she is successful, the success is not necessarily as good as it could be, in spite of tremendous amount of talent and effort expended toward the job.

Personal Quadrant—F.

Works long hours; does not have much time to develop and maintain good personal relationships. Does not organize her limited spare time efficiently.

Health Quadrant—F.

Doesn't have much time to bother about herself; tends not to get enough exercise, or even take time to eat properly.

Job Quadrant—S.

As recognized by all peers, in awe of her sheer commitment, "could not possibly be doing a better job." However is probably past her peak efficiency level with *too much* unremitting stress.

Final Score—2 Fs.

Predictable decrease in quality and quantity of life. It is not good enough to excel only in one or two quadrants. Workaholics not only cheat themselves of a longer life, but deny themselves a better life.

It is important to realize that the success scale is dynamic. It changes with different stages in your life, so it should be constantly kept in mind. Test yourself often. Remember, Howard Hughes and Marilyn Monroe were successful in their earlier years. A major key to success is balance. If you are an absolute failure in even one quadrant, this will ultimately weaken your successes in the other three, and can reduce your life expectancy in the future and the quality of your life today.

Use the following report card to try to assess yourself. Be flexible enough to invest some effort in areas of failure, if you find any.

Your report card

Enter your name here.

	S	F
1. Financial		
2. Personal		
3. Health		
4. Job (or Education)		
Your Final Score		

If you scored *any* **Fs**, beware!

A showdown with poverty: Will you win or lose?

There is no question that poverty increases stress, primarily by decreasing one's control over situations. However, this is not say it is impossible to experience the "Joy of Stress," though poor. The key is still the same—trying to gain control by organization.

Case history—David F.

Aged forty, unemployed executive, suddenly laid off. After a few weeks of failed job interviews, depression sets in. Along with this comes a decrease in self-image, which then leads to a decrease in sales ability—most particularly, the ability to sell himself. He ends up doing odd jobs around the house, and doing a few extra odd jobs for relatives. However, he can't be bothered doing this kind of thing for money, even though he has obvious skills. He could use his carpentry, gardening, electrical, and other general "fix-it" abilities in a productive way to help tide him over, and at least give him some measure of self-confidence.

Instead, he starts smoking, drinking more, vegetating in front of the soap operas during daytime TV, arguing more with his wife, and basically getting worse. This shows the *power of negative thinking,* and demonstrates that disorganization can cause predictable increase in stress.

Case history—John B.

Aged forty, unemployed executive, suddenly laid off, but is a *positive thinker.* Takes stock of what has happened; reassesses his true abilities, strengths, weaknesses, and priorities, including his minimum needs for salary, and his flexibility. Does market research; finds what skills are best to emphasize in the marketplace. He ends up moving to a new town, and settles for blue-collar work but, with overtime, makes almost what he made before. After a year, he gets into a better job as a marketing executive for a new company.

John B. is flexible, willing to change locations or style as required. He is not committed to spending the rest of his days in a ghost town, or in an obsolete profession. This is a classic example of how positive thinking can take the bad effects of negative stress, and turn them around into productive, useful responses.

10.
Hanson's Three Principles of Stress Management

1. Pamper yourself.
2. Stop stonewalling.
3. Face the truth.

Hanson's First Principle of Stress Management:

1. Pamper yourself (within your budget)

Frequent small rewards (not necessarily expensive) are far more effective than one big reward after years of sacrifice. We all know this in the sense in which it relates to raising our pets and our children. However, tragically, I see case after case in my office of adults who ignore this principle themselves with uniformly predictable results. The one common thread is that in every such case, the person totally underestimates the importance and value of his or her *spare* time.

The daily small reward, whether it is a game of tennis or reading in a hot bath, is the way to stay fresh and on top of your stresses each day. Stoic sacrifices for long periods of time, waiting for just one big reward, weaken you for stresses and undermine your efficiency, thus forming a vicious circle. Some actual case histories will help to illustrate.

1. One patient, whose dream and big reward was to be her own boss at all costs, quit a good job as a sales clerk to open her own shop. She did it prematurely and without adequate market research. As a result, she has gone the past eight years without being able to afford any of her former little rewards, such as holidays, or even the simplest treat. Her health,

*F*rankly, poverty rots. An adequate supply of money properly used can give you some control over your life. It can even buy happiness in the form of increasing your resistance to stress. (See Chapter 4.)

It is not necessary to be rich, but simply to have room in your budget for improving stress reduction measures. Often, substantial sums of money are being wasted on measures guaranteed to make matters worse, such as gambling, highly speculative investments, poor lifestyle choices (for example, over-eating, smoking, and excessive alcohol consumption), or simply disorganized and reckless spending habits.

which she took for granted and undervalued, is now beginning to crack.

2. A patient, who was a commission salesman, needed a large deck on the back of his house; he enjoyed a little carpentry. He decided to do all the work himself rather than hire professionals. He eventually finished it, but in the process he regretted wasting quality evening and weekend hours with his wife and kids. Even putting forth his best effort, he could not possibly build the deck as efficiently as an experienced contractor, and ended up taking half the summer on the project. To make matters worse, he had to leave work early to do carpentry, and fell far behind in sending out his account billing, thus losing more money in interest payments than he saved on the deck. Clearly, the Big Reward (a cheap deck) was not worth the loss of frequent small rewards (enjoying the family).

3. A couple working different shifts spent too great a portion of their income on a fancy house, and were unable to afford baby sitters or to spend money on their own entertainment. They totally undervalued their spare time, which became devoted to tag-team baby sitting. They rarely saw their friends, and predictably grew to resent the house, the kids, and even each other.

4. Bob and Jane, a working couple wanted the Big Reward of getting out of debt quickly. They thus decided to put Bob's salary in the bank, and live on just Jane's salary. After ten years of frugality, including the last six years with no proper vacation, Bob started to feel burnt out at his job as a contractor. He lost his former energy and hustle, and began to work

less efficiently. His business declined, and he ended up bankrupt.

Big rewards can have pretty steep price tags in terms of stress. Taking the frequent small reward principle even further, it should be pointed out that such rewards are best given during the course of each *day.* In fact, many stress-reducing rewards have now been incorporated into the average household, for example, disposable diapers, instant hot water, frozen meals, and Dial-a-Joke.

Hanson's Second and Third Principles of Stress Management:

2. Stop stonewalling—Ignore all those comforting but uncontrollable excuses.
3. Face the truth—Worry effectively about only those things you can control.

With reflex swiftness, people in difficulty "stonewall," or place the blame for their problems and stresses on the nearest uncontrollable excuse; something they can't change. But if you train yourself to look behind this comforting stone wall, you will find the *true* cause of your problems (often painful to face), which you *can* control *if* you face them. Truly uncontrollable causes of stress, such as natural disasters and genuine bad luck, are fortunately rare, although they are likely to completely fill the news media headlines.

Reacting to a problem by this "stonewall-ing" is a doubly bad way to handle stress. It allows you to call off the hunt and stop looking for the real culprit; or it may have you losing sleep worrying about things that are simply beyond your sphere of influence.

Let's examine some common problems you might encounter in each of the four quadrants of your life. Note that *in every case* you can defeat the stresses only by facing the *truth* behind each knee-jerk excuse that pops up. Energy and time spent on worrying about the uncontrollable are totally wasted.

When you think of recipients of the most preposterous excuses, you would probably head the list with priests who hear confessions and traffic cops who issue speeding tickets. How-ever, it is the family doctor who gets to hear some of the truly world-class excuses.

For each of the problems listed below, I have heard patients "stonewall" or blame all of their comfortable, uncontrollable excuses. It is only when I get them to face the *truth* (however unpleasant it might appear) that they can see how to control and solve their own problems.

This makes all the difference between win-ning and losing your stress battles.

Financial Quadrant

*Problem: Not enough money no matter what
I earn (relative poverty).*

Stonewall	**Face the Truth**
"Bad economy."	Unrealistic goals.
"Inflation."	Living on your gross income, not your net.
"High interest rates."	Inefficient spending habits.
"It's society's fault, so I just shrug and put up with it."	Insufficient shopping around. Impulsive spender; competitive response to peer pressure (for example, keeping up with the Joneses).
"I'm too tired to bother hustling at work."	Sometimes it takes money to make money. By hiring out part-time work around the house, you can spend more effective time at work, and have more efficient relaxation with your family in your off-hours. This "recharging of the battery" process is often underrated, but can lead to greater financial gain in the end. Remember Hanson's First Principle of Stress Reduction—Pamper Yourself.

Personal Quadrant

Problem: Marriage drifting apart.

Stonewall

Face the Truth

"She's bored at home."

The truth is, she is under-stimulated, overtrained for the job, and quite possibly disorganized. Probably suffering from *too little* stress (see page xx), and would benefit from taking on extra duties outside the home.

"Can't talk about anything controversial with spouse."

Poor communication; fear of the big "door slamming" arguments. (Before resorting to this kind of theatrics, check out the construction of your front door. Many modern lightweight insulated doors make a most unsatisfactory "biff" sound. This somewhat undermines the effect on the slammee.)

Poor communication is an example of the power of negative thinking. By dwelling on all of the negative reactions to a controversial subject, one can imagine a wide variety of unpleasant conclusions. As a result, couples often go on for decades without ever communicating on key issues. They end up suffering far more than just the few moments of unpleasantness that they were originally afraid to face.

"He never takes me out for dinner."	He has seven thousand calories for lunch on his expense account.
He (she) is a workaholic.	Disorganized at work, ego trip, or classic avoidance of potential conflicts at home. An easy "copout," which in most professions is seen to be socially acceptable, even admirable. From the point of view of the spouse who is left behind, it's no better than spending an evening out gambling or playing poker every night.
He (she) needs "head space."	He/she is out to lunch.
He (she) "needs someone younger."	Hasn't been getting any lately. Trying to recapture his/her youth, which certainly can be done. The only problem is that it is never his/her *own* youth.
All the "fun has gone."	Inflexibility in your routine, no room left for spontaneity. She is not crazy about forty-two hours of TV football every weekend. He is a little tired of hearing about the afternoon soap operas at dinner.

Problem: Sex life a "yawn."

Stonewall   **Face the Truth**

"What else can you expect at my age?"	Anxiety and stress, including boredom. It is important to remember that anxiety in the man

212

results in an earlier climax, even to the extent of premature ejaculation, whereas the same anxiety in a woman delays her orgasm time, which means she may not even be getting warmed up before he is cooled off. This is one of the most common disparities in sex life. It can be directly controlled. Marriage counseling is often helpful here, along with reading such books as *The Joy of Sex* by Alex Comfort and *Human Sexual Inadequacy* by Masters and Johnson.

Problem: Your kids have become strangers.

Stonewall

Face the Truth

Teenage surliness.

Insufficient quality time invested in getting to know them as they grew. A classic problem of Type A workaholics. Often seen in those children whose parents misguidedly try to *spare* their children from facing stress.

"I never seem to have enough time to spend with the family."

Probably disorganized, trying to do too much without efficient delegation. May need to decline some nonessential activities at work and at home, for example, volunteer groups, committee work, and extra business ventures. This is typical of people who have passed their peak on the Joy of Stress graph (see Chapter 1), and suffer *too much* stress.

Health Quadrant

Problem: Chest pains.

Stonewall	**Face the Truth**

"It will pass." "Probably something I ate."

Potential warning of heart attack—do not ignore. Sixty percent of self-employed businessmen experience some form of chest pains, and most ignore it. Consult your doctor for a thorough physical examination, and ignore the pains only after the doctor has concluded they are not serious. Do not come to this conclusion yourself.

Problem: Poor exercise tolerance.

Stonewall	**Face the Truth**
"It's just my age."	Total sloth since age six.
"I do play softball."	For all but two minutes per game, you are leaning on your knees waiting for the ball to come.
"I do bowl regularly."	The pins get more exercise than you do.
"I play a little touch football on the weekends."	Sounds like a beer commercial, and in fact the calories gained from the post-game beers usually negate the benefits gained in the exercise in the first place.

Problem: Obesity.

Stonewall	Face the Truth
"The food is there when I prepare it for my family, so I eat it."	If you can train your dog not to jump up on the counter and eat the family's food, you should be able to train yourself.
"My weight just seems to stay where it is."	You have to eat bags of groceries each week just to keep your weight up there. Remember, obesity is not passive; it requires *active* overeating.
"I eat less than all my friends."	That's only when they are watching; on your own you eat like crazy.
"I only eat to be polite. People often say, 'Eat this; I made it especially for you!'" 	This may be sabotage or manipulation by spouse, parents, or peers who resent your success. It can be evidence of jealousy. People may prefer to keep you in a nonthreatening, fat condition. Recognize the technique for what it is, and politely but firmly decline. Agreeing to overeat may be just a manifestation of poor self-image.
"I have to bake (or buy treats) for the kids."	Let's face it. You bake (or buy) for yourself, and the kids just get what you can't eat.
"I'm big boned."	Big bones won't explain why you stick to a plastic chair. You are *fat*. Until you admit it, you will never lose weight. Depending on bone structure, there may well be leeway for an extra ten or fifteen pounds

above the "ideal" weight. Taking the bathing suit test in front of a full-length mirror will tell you if you have any rolls of fat to spare.

"I eat out at restaurants a lot."

Just because you are not washing the dishes doesn't mean you have to eat everything on the menu.

"It's certainly *not because I overeat."*

It *certainly* is.

Poor self-image or lack of confidence; fear of being hurt.

Getting fat is simply an avoidance technique to avoid being vulnerable to social hurts. Often it indicates cowardice. If you treat yourself with more respect, you will find others will do so as well.

"I can't exercise because I'm too heavy, or my back hurts, or my knees hurt."

Try swimming. Even a hippopotamus is graceful under water.

"It's glandular."

It's not. You overeat.

"It's breakfast time, so I must eat breakfast (substitute "lunch" or "dinner" for this comment as well)."

For the obese, skipping a meal is perfectly OK if you are not hungry.

"I have to prepare the food for my whole family; that's why I get fat."

You wouldn't have to prepare as much food if you didn't eat it as fast as you made it.

"I get weak if I don't have something in my stomach."

If a brown bear can go all winter without food, you should be able to hang in there for another two hours until dinner. If you really feel you need something in your stomach, try a low-calorie, high-fiber snack. (See Figure 5.2 and Appendix C.)

"It's hereditary."	Your whole family overeats.
"I just have to look at food . . ."	*". . . and then eat it."*
"Obesity runs in my family."	*Nobody* runs in your family.

Problem: Smoking.

Stonewall

Face the Truth

"It relaxes me."

So does waving goodbye to your mother-in-law.

"I gain weight if I quit."

Get a pacifier. Many smokers end up with a weight problem as well. The real problem is the oral urge, retained from the thumb-sucking stage of childhood.

"Nobody can stand me when I'm in withdrawal."

Such behavioral problems can be controlled. See your doctor; try hypnosis or acupuncture, if necessary.

"I can't quit now because there is a big meeting coming up soon, and everyone will be smoking."

This is procrastination. After one meeting will come another, and so on. Do it today!

"It gives me something to do with my hands at a party."

So does picking your nose.

"It makes me look sophisticated and confident to others."

Your sports jacket reeks so much it could set off a smoke alarm from fifty paces.

"It's romantic."

Your breath smells like a baked sneaker.

Problem: Excessive drinking.

Stonewall ***Face the Truth***

"Peer pressure."

Have you ever thought of trying new peers? If you continue excessive drinking, the well-known diuretic effect of alcohol upon your kidneys might well help you become one of the great "pee-ers" of our time.

"Stress at work (or at home)."

It seems easier to try to drown your stresses than to face them directly. But turning tail and running isn't going to make your stresses disappear; only facing up to them is.

Problem: Skin wrinkles especially on the face.

Stonewall ***Face the Truth***

"It's just my age."

There are three preventable causes of the aging of the skin that account for most wrinkles.

1. Excess Sun.
Even by your early twenties, your face could start to look like the back of a cowboy's neck. Quite apart from the risks of skin cancer, a great number of "sun spots" may be splattered all over your skin, and could make you look as if you came last in a horse race. Direct sun rays will also cause the skin to become thinner and more friable. All of these changes are totally controllable with the simple use of appropriate

clothing, sun blocks, a big hat, or sitting in the shade.

2. Excess Alcohol.

Taking excesses of alcohol each day brings about aging of the skin, and for that matter advanced aging of the rest of the body as well. (See Chapter 3.)

3. Excess Stress.

Can almost age a person "overnight."

Problem: Tension headaches.

Stonewall

Face the Truth

"Just too much stress."

Failure to gain control of your problems. Lack of relaxation skills that would often be able to abort a headache attack at the onset (easily learned by hypnosis or a number of other methods, see *Power Nap,* page 94). Poor dietary choices, such as too much sugar, resulting in rebound hypoglycemic headache, trigger headache. Allergies, for example, to shellfish, peanuts, some dairy products. (Consult your doctor to help identify them.)

These may be from the rebound headache phenomenon, from taking too much in the way of medications for the previous headache. This can become a vicious cycle, and is particularly seen when people are on strong doses of codeine for their headaches.

In any event, all headaches should be given full respect, and investigated thoroughly by your doctor. Albeit rarely, simple headache could be the sign of a much more serious underlying problem, and thus must not be ignored.

I have found that through the use of acupuncture many people have been able to get off chronic high doses of their medications. Once freed from the pain-medication cycle, these patients frequently find that their headaches abate.

Problem: Miscellaneous—eczema, high blood pressure, and so on.

Often directly related to stress, and thus can respond to improved stress management in their treatment plans. See your doctor.

Job Quadrant

Problem: Business failed (self-employed).

Stonewall	Face the Truth
"It's the weather."	That's what you get for starting the only sod farm in Death Valley.
"It's the interest rates."	Wrong marketing, wrong location. Wrong timing, for example, patio furniture in October, or wrong product, such as corner cupboards to Eskimos. Mismanagement of self and staff through incompetence, or simply by not having the correct skills for the job.
"It's the bank's fault; they called my loan."	Banks are not supposed to be bottomless pits of charity. In most cases, banks want to *keep* lending you money, unless you make them fear you may default.
"I was just ahead of my time" (implying a hidden compliment to yourself).	You had absolutely no sense of timing whatsoever.
"My customers didn't understand my product" (implying they were the stupid ones).	Either you didn't explain and market the product properly, or you chose the wrong product. (Either way, this implies that you were to blame.)

221

Problem: Laid off, for example, because of plant closing.

Stonewall	Face the Truth

"It's the recession."

There may be a number of things that can help. There is no need to remain in a "ghost town" if work is available in other parts of the country. The USA, for instance, was founded by people who realized this when work was scarce in Europe.

"There's nothing we can do about it."

It is helpful to be flexible enough to move to better areas to find work, retrain skills, or come down a peg and do lesser work for a while. (One of my patients was a skilled research scientist in an obscure area of metallurgy. When the plant closed in his town in a remote area, he was able to move successfully to the industrial belt, and obtain employment on the assembly line in a large auto plant. His earnings, with overtime, ended up being about the same as before. His colleagues, who were inflexible and refused to look for anything other than their specialty, are still unemployed and suffering much more severe stress.)

Many unemployed could still do part-time "odd jobs" in the neighborhood; for example, cutting grass, shoveling snow, painting. This might at least keep the wolves from the door while the person is looking for something more suitable. Or it could even lead into a full-time business. In all but the most severely depressed areas of the country, there is usually a good underground market for this type of work.

Problem: Executive demoted or fired.

Stonewall

Face the Truth

"I blame the system."
"I was stabbed in the back."
"I was fired because I'm over fifty."
"I was fired because I don't have a university education."

Could be poor performance or interpersonal politics. Skills and personal needs may not be keeping up with the company's needs.

Problem: Can't find work after Ph.D.

Stonewall

Face the Truth

"Nobody is hiring these days."

Nobody is hiring unless you have a saleable skill. A Ph.D. in ancient English literature is unlikely to excite many boardroom recruiters in big business.

Problem: Few friends at work.

Stonewall

Face the Truth

"Nobody worth knowing."

They probably think the same of you. Friendships need to be worked at and nurtured. If you have a couple of good friends, then you need not worry about having everyone else in your most intimate circle.

Problem: Bored at work; hate job.

Stonewall

Face the Truth

"That's the way everyone feels—that's life."

Could be a classic Peter Principle case—getting promoted until incompetent; then stopping there.

Corollary of this is that, in any given hierarchy, all will be tending toward incompetence. Solution—know thyself; refuse any promotion that takes you from something you excel at to something you don't do well. Ask for *demotion* if necessary. In an excellent company, your wishes will be granted; in an incompetent company you may be forced to quit.

"Up to my ears at work—but nobody else could do the work as well."

Poor teacher and poor delegater. Couldn't even organize a two-car funeral.

Problem: Too much stress from my job.

Stonewall

Face the Truth

"I hate my job, but I can't leave for another ten years because I'll lose my pension."

You don't have to spend all your life in the wrong job, or for that matter in the wrong marriage or relationships with friends. Nor do you have to make poor choices in resistance to stress, which will almost predetermine the mechanical breakdown of some part of your body. You're not a mindless lump of lead, which, being shot out of a cannon, waits simply for its time to fall to the ground. You can fly, and steer your own destiny.

"My pension guarantees that I'll enjoy my retirement."

How much good is a pension to your widow? Probably she'd rather have *you*.

Money is no guarantee you will enjoy your retirement. Don't simply contrast your negative feelings about your (wrong) job with the positive feelings you think you will have upon retiring.

You could quit the job you hate today, and start a new career at something you love. Even if your financial intake were a little less, you could work at it for more years, enjoy each *day* in the process, and be less likely to die from too little stress (within two years of an idle retirement—see page xix).

Conclusion

Now that you have read this book, you should be fully aware of the stresses that pervade your life. You should also know how to build your defenses into a virtual fortress. You know what goes on in your body when you are under attack from stress. You also know that your body's reflex reactions by themselves are no longer completely appropriate or adequate, but can be consciously strengthened by the aware defender. The battle lines are drawn; victory is yours for the taking. The costs are negligible; the sacrifices few. The rewards are richer than any lottery, can be drawn upon each day, and accrue the added bonus of a prolonged useful life and greater financial profits in your business.

If you exercise your control competently and make the correct decisions in your response to stress, the odds will be "stacked" heavily in your favor. If you ignore this advice, you may bumble into an easily avoidable ambush, and uselessly squander the gift of intelligence, which elevates human beings from the animal kingdom.

So do not look to the future with a fatalistic shrug. Get involved with the fight for your life, and win. Don't hide from stresses; go out and challenge new ones. Take the *thrill* from stress, but leave the *threat* behind. Start your offense right now. See how gratifying the unbeatable combination of a properly maintained body and a well-organized mind can be. Be justifiably optimistic about your future. Take an active role in your own management; do not be just a passive tourist through life.

Follow Hanson's Three Principles of Stress Management:
1. Pamper yourself.
2. Stop stonewalling.
3. Face the truth.

Best of all, the Hanson method requires only that you seek a life of greater fulfillment, flavor, and fun—for your own sake and for the sake of those who love you.

Now you know THE JOY OF STRESS.

Afterword

Life Is Not So Simple:
A personal illustration

*Now, I know what you are thinking. Life is not
so simple. Although all this analysis of stress in
your body is logical, the impediment of human
frailty, and the occasion itself, can oft combine to
trip you up. Well, you're right. No one is
immune. . . .*

During a summer I spent in England as a
young medical student, a friendly local wine
merchant suggested he arrange some "hospitality" at one of the top champagne chateaus in
France.

Expecting to be tagging onto the end of a
conducted tour, I was surprised to find one of
the officers of the company waiting for me personally. We spent a couple of hours sipping
through miles of underground caves stacked
with champagne bottles.

I was then escorted into a special reception
room built in honor of one of Napoleon's frequent visits to "tank up" before battle. White-
gloved valets in uniforms with gold braid
flanked the room. There were four chairs set
around the enormous table, all at one end. The
charming Comptesse de Maigre, the owner of
Moët et Chandon, walked into the room and

shook my hand. She was followed by a younger countess, and one of the senior executives. With the encouragement of the side waiters, more champagne flowed. "Far be it from me turn down a free drink at this stage of my life," thought I.

After an hour I was getting significantly impaired. None of my hosts showed even the slightest sign of intoxication—a tribute to the training and fortitude of the Gallic liver. I was requested to follow them along for lunch. I followed the procession of shiny cars, jerking along in my rented Simca. We drove up about a mile of treed driveway, through the stone archway into the courtyard of the magnificent Chateau de Saran, once a hunting castle used by the kings of France.

A platoon of military-style servants marched out to greet the convoy, each one opening a car door. Mine took out my duffel bag, and then ushered me into the chateau. I was helped up to my large corner room. Its draped windows were at least eight feet tall, and gave onto the courtyard. My valet explained with a bit of a sigh that only recently Bridgette Bardot had slept in the same bed, but had just departed. I shared this disappointing news with him, but told him to cheer up—that she might still have a chance to meet me somewhere else.

I then washed my face in cold water, in a vain attempt to sober up. Within five minutes I reported downstairs for pre-lunch drinks. A sumptuous lunch was served, with three kinds of wine. It concluded with several cognacs. Suppressing a belch, I tried to get my eyes to focus as the countess suggested I should now drive to Chateau Mercier, a smaller house of very fine champagne.

At the Chateau Mercier, I was greeted by
the manager, in an Imperial museum room. As
I was his only visitor, what could I do but
accept the hospitality of yet another free bottle
of champagne? My only recollection of the tour
that followed was that we were traveling at some
speed in an electric golf cart, my hair was
standing straight out behind me, my tie was
over both shoulders, and millions of bottles and
casks were flying by me at low altitude.

I staggered back upstairs with the steady-
ing assistance of the manager. Before bidding
me adieu, he poured me a parting glass of
champagne. It was now five minutes to eight as
I was being helped into my car. The last
instructions that I had remembered from the
countess were to make sure I was back to the
chateau by eight o'clock, for a very important
formal dinner with the Swiss ambassador.

I proceeded to drive down the road for ten
minutes, and got lost. Out of panic born of
stress, I finally found a single light on in the
upstairs part of an unfinished house. I negoti-
ated my way through an obstacle course of
construction debris, managed to somehow
climb up a ladder, and inquire as to the location
of the bloody chateau. The occupant pointed
directly up the hill, and my arm followed his—
both pointing in the same direction.

However, as I turned around to go down
the ladder, my arm was pointing in the opposite
direction. Much to my informant's dismay, that
was the direction in which I proceeded.

About fifteen minutes later, I was fran-
tically doing large ovals in a jungle of snarled
grapevines, the car getting ever deeper in the
mud. Finally I saw a light through the thicket

and managed to skid my way toward it, drag-
ging half the vines behind me. I knocked upon
the window to find out where the chateau was.
Much to my surprise the person who greeted
me at the window was the countess herself. I
was at the back door of the garden room, and
the formal party was in full progress. I brushed
myself off, did up my tweed sports jacket, and
then confidently followed her in. She had me at
her elbow as she escorted me around the room,
and very kindly introduced me to all of the
dinner guests. I remember bleating some asi-
nine apology for my condition, based on the
fact that there was a five-hour time difference
between North America and France—although
the countess had just mentioned that I had been
in Europe for a month.

More champagne was poured, and then the
military butler announced that dinner was
served. As I explained to the guests and the
Swiss ambassador, I was now feeling a tad tired.
I suggested that it might be appropriate for me
to have a quick nap before joining them for the
rest of the dinner. I then excused myself and
very calmly walked up the stairs and got into
bed.

That at any rate is what I thought had happened. Apparently, the scene in reality went as
follows. When I crashed in through the back
door, the right knee of my pants had been completely torn down to the ankle. I had mud all
over my tie, and completely filling one shoe.
My jacket had been done up on the wrong button. I lurched with a "step, squish, step," over
all of the priceless carpets, leaning heavily on
the countess.

When I bade my elegant adieux, apparently I climbed only five stairs, then slid back

four, uttered a loud oath, and then climbed another ten stairs, slid back six, cursed, and climbed again. No one in the room could even talk due to the din echoing through the stone hall.

When I finally got to the top of the stairs, everyone could hear me hanging over the great white telephone, calling for "Ralph" and "Hewie." Much to my horror, when I woke up the following morning and peered onto the courtyard below, I found the contemptible Simca totally covered in mud, blocking the rear driveway, and wearing half the vines of the House of Moët. There was a jack under the left front, and the white-gloved guard was very disdainfully trying to remove the ribbons of what had once been a tire. He managed to place the spare tire on it, but gave a look that implied he would rather have been cleaning out elephant stables.

After addressing my headache problem with a couple of aspirins, neither of which worked, I finally dared to show my face downstairs for breakfast. The countess offered her sincere sympathy, noting that most foreigners had rather a bad time of it, as they were not used to drinking. As I was leaving, the countess very warmly invited me to come back and take another run at it. As a parting gesture to try to make me feel better, she noted that the month before they had misplaced an entire bus tour of forty Japanese, who had apparently taken the wrong track after the wine tasting and got lost behind a hedge.

■

Appendix A

"Know Thyself":

Social style quadrants

As we have seen, good stress management requires accurate personal assessment. There are many reasons for this, such as in choosing *realistic goals* (Chapter 4), finding the right sort of *job* for your aptitudes, and in providing a basis for understanding your boss, employees, clients, and most importantly, your spouse and children.

A simple, yet remarkably consistent guide-line to the recognition of four basic styles of behavior has been devised for sales people by Larry Wilson, of the Larry Wilson Learning Corp.

While originally devised to teach a salesperson to be versatile, and have *completely different* approaches to each of the four styles, the same versatility can be a great help in daily interpersonal relations. Each style or quadrant feels most *comfortable* with its own approaches to a problem. In the workplace, most people instinctively get along well with others in the same quadrant. For some reason, however, people rarely marry a spouse from the same quadrant. Although this does add some element of zing to a marriage, failure to learn this versatility, and to recognize each other's needs and desires can lead to great marital friction. I have found this system to be an invaluable aid in marital counseling, in helping people understand why others behave as they do.

These styles are only matters of comfort and preference, and have nothing to do with intelligence, ambition, or success. However, with each style come predictable patterns of behavior. Knowing them will greatly improve your understanding of others, and your interpersonal relations at home and at work will benefit.

First let's see where you fit, then assess those around you. There are only two questions you need to ask: 1) Is the subject *responsive?*, and 2) is the subject *assertive?* See chart 1 for guidelines to recognition.

Once you have identified your main quadrant (most people have lesser tendencies to at least one other quadrant) then check on chart 2 to find out your predictable patterns or tendencies. This chart is used by a trained *(versatile)* salesperson in knowing how best to present his or her product to the people in each quadrant. (See bibliography.)

Check the quadrant of your spouse, children, and parents to see if you can better understand how they approach a problem, and see if you can reduce stress at home by becoming more versatile in your relationships with them.

These same skills can help reduce stress at work; not just by increasing sales, but by being able to better understand how to stimulate an employee to greater productivity, and how to improve relations with your boss.

Finally, in reference to those who may have the wrong job, see chart 3 to see if your social style has predetermined your failure. Use this knowledge to select a more appropriate line of work. (This is particularly helpful to your children. when they are at the stage of choosing their own lines of study and career.)

Chart Ia

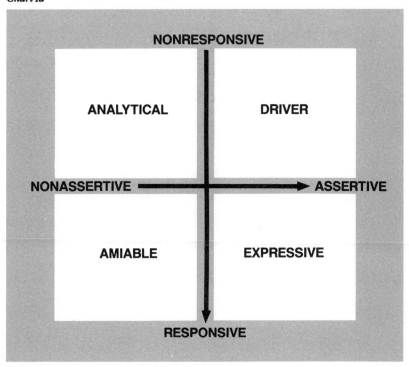

© Wilson Learning Corp. 1978

Guideline for Recognition

How Responsive Is the Person?

Nonresponsive

Reserved, unresponsive, poker face
Actions cautious or careful
Wants facts and details
Eye contact infrequent while listening
Eyes harsh, severe or serious
Limited personal feelings, story telling or small
    talk

How Assertive Is the Person?

Nonassertive

Few uses of voice to
   emphasize ideas
Expressions and
   posture are quiet
   and submissive
Deliberate, studied, or
   slow in speech
Indifferent handshake
Asks questions more
   often than makes
   statements
Vague, unclear about
   what is wanted
Tends to lean
   backwards

Assertive

Emphasizes ideas by
   tone change
Expressions are
   aggressive or
   dominant
Quick, clear or fast
   paced
Firm handshake
Makes statements
   more often than
   asks questions
Lets one know what is
   wanted
Tends to lean forward
   to make a point

Responsive

Animated, uses facial expressions
Smiles, nods, frowns
Actions open or eager
Little effort to push for facts
Eye contact frequent while listening
Friendly gaze
Hands free, palms up, open
Friendly gestures
Shares personal feelings
Attentive, responsive, enjoys the relationship

Strengths and Weaknesses

Chart 2	PERCEIVED STRENGTHS	PERCEIVED WEAKNESSES
Driver (Control Specialist)	Determined Tough-minded Decisive Efficient Takes charge	Pushy Severe Dominating Harsh Demanding
Expressive (Social Specialist)	Personable Stimulating Enthusiastic Dramatic Inspiring	Opinionated Manipulating Excitable Reacting Promotional
Amiable (Support Specialist)	Supportive Respectful Willing Dependable Personable	Conforming Retiring Noncommital Undisciplined Emotional
Analytical (Technical Specialist)	Industrious Persistent Serious Vigilant Orderly	Uncommunicative Indecisive Cool Exacting Impersonal

© Wilson Learning Corp. 1978

Chart 3	RIGHT TYPE OF JOB	WRONG TYPE OF JOB
Driver	Business or political leader.	Baby photographer.
Expressive	Actor, PR, sales— Anything with a lot of public contact.	Accountant, research scientist, librarian.
Amiable	PR, sales, service, industry	Bill collector, union leader, marine drill sergeant, bouncer.
Analytical	Accountant, stock market analyst, researcher, physicist.	Game show host, entertainment (fun) coordinator on a cruise ship.

Social Style Summary Chart

MASTER CHART USED BY SALES PERSONNEL:	DRIVER
STYLE WHEN BACKED "INTO A CORNER"	Autocratic
MEASURES PERSONAL VALUE BY	Results
FOR GROWTH NEEDS TO	Listen
LET THEM SAVE	Time
NEEDS CLIMATE THAT	Allows to build own structure
TAKE TIME TO BE	Efficient
SUPPORT THEIR	Conclusions & Actions
GIVE BENEFITS THAT ANSWER	What
FOR DECISIONS GIVE THEM	Options & Probabilities
SPECIALTY	Control

© Wilson Learning Corp. 1978

EXPRESSIVE	AMIABLE	ANALYTICAL
Attacker	Acquiescer	Avoider
Applause	Attention	Activity
Check	Reach	Decide
Effort	Relationships	Face
Inspires to their goals	Provides details	Suggests
Stimulating	Agreeable	Accurate
Dreams & Intuitions	Relationships & Feelings	Principles & Thinking
Who	Why	How
Testimony & Incentives	Guarantees & Assurances	Evidence & Service
Social	Supportive	Technical

Appendix B

Vitamin and Mineral Chart

Fat Soluble Vitamins

Stored in large quantities in the body; supplements rarely tend to be needed.

Vitamin A

Functions: Important to maintain the health of skin and inner linings of the body. Essential for vision and integrity of part of the eye structure. Vitamin A also aids resistance to infection. Essential for many of the body's chemical functions.

Found In: Carrots, spinach, turnip greens, and other vegetables, palm oil, dairy products, eggs, and so on. High doses of vitamin A are found in liver. However, as inhabitants of the Far North are aware, fish livers and polar bear livers are generally to be avoided. They may contain poisonously high levels of vitamin A.

How Much Do We Need? 5,000 international units (IU) per day for an adult, easily obtained from a sensible diet. Anything in excess of this will be stored in the liver, up to its maximum capacity. After this, excesses of the vitamin will be released into the bloodstream with poisonous and ultimately fatal side effects.

Vitamin D

Functions: Prevents rickets; essential to the absorption of calcium from the intestines, and for normal bone growth and development. (Without sufficient vitamin D, there will be inadequate absorption of calcium from foods, and calcium will be mobilized from the bone into the bloodstream to make up deficiencies.) Abnormal deposits of calcium will be made in some bones. Unless corrected early by a vitamin D supply, victims will be permanently crippled. In adults, vitamin D deficiency produces a softening of the bones, which causes great pain and deformity.

Found In: Fish, egg yolks, butter, cheese, and milk; and in the livers of beef, pork, and lamb. However, most adults obtain all or most of their vitamin D requirement from the action of sunlight on the skin. The fortification of milk with vitamin D has been instrumental in providing adequate sources of this vitamin for North American children.

How Much Do We Need? 400 international units (IU) per day for children and pregnant or lactating women. The requirement for children drops to 200 IU after the age of twenty-two. Supplements are usually not needed.

Vitamin E

Functions: An antioxidant important in preventing destructive attack by oxygen on the essential unsaturated fat in cell membranes, as well as protecting vitamin A in the intestines. It also helps to maintain muscle metabolism. It maintains the health of heart muscle, blood vessels, liver, kidney tubules, brain cells, and so on. Vitamin E deficiency impairs the production of sperm in males, and increases fetal loss during pregnancy in females.

Found In: Vegetable oils, most vegetables, many fruits, eggs, dairy products.

How Much Do We Need? Ten to fifteen international units (IU) per day for adults, but more may be needed when under stress and in certain other situations. People seem to be able to consume megadoses without many side effects. However, taking excesses will eventually lead to significant accumulation in the body, in the fatty tissues. The harmful effects of long-term continuation of high doses are not fully known. It is safest to keep your intake of Vitamin E below 100 IU per day.

Vitamin K

Functions: Needed primarily for blood clotting mechanism, to protect from internal bleeding or bleeding from cuts and wounds.

Found In: Green leafy vegetables, soybeans, many other vegetables, beef liver, green tea, egg yolks, dairy products.

How Much Do We Need? Some 70 to 140 micrograms per day. However, a normal diet typically provides about 400 micrograms per day. Thus supplementation is unnecessary, except in a few unusual cases. Your doctor can advise you as to whether you need extra vitamin K.

Water Soluble Vitamins

Soluble in water; thus excreted in urine daily; constant regular supply needed.

Vitamin B1 (Thiamin)

Functions: Prevention of beriberi, which is characterized by a slow, increasing weakness. Also essential for the functioning of nerve tissue, heart muscles, and energy supplies to the body.

Found In: Natural brown rice, as well as all lean meats, eggs, milk, and seafoods. It is also found to a lesser extent in most fruits and vegetables. Historically, in Asia, where rice is a major food in the diet, the very poor have tended to escape beriberi. Unlike the rich, they could not afford the processed "refined" rice, which was depleted of all thiamin (as well as fiber).

How Much Do We Need? Approximately 1.5 mg for an adult. Supplements of greater amounts than this are not toxic. Most vitamin supplement pills contain 15 to 20 mg.

Vitamin B2 (Riboflavin)

Functions: Essential for maintenance of the skin, mucous membranes, cornea, nerves.

Found In: Milk and other dairy products, liver, kidneys, fruits, and vegetables. Milk supplies nearly 40 percent of the riboflavin in the Western diet, along with bread and cereals.

How Much Do We Need? 1.3 to 1.7 mg for an adult. There is no known toxicity of megadoses of this vitamin.

Niacin, or Nicotinic Acid (Formerly called Vitamin B3 or B4)

Functions: Prevention of pellagra, which used to be a significant problem resulting from eating an imbalanced diet. Classically pellagra involves dermatitis, diarrhea, dementia, and even death.

Found In: Meats, and to a lesser extent, grains, fruits, and vegetables, along with milk and eggs.

How Much Do We Need? About 20 mg per day for an adult. Doses of nicotinic acid above 500 mg can be harmful. In its niacinamide form, it can be taken in doses up to 4,000 mg without fear. (But this dose is not necessary.)

Vitamin B6 (Pyrodoxine)

Functions: Essential for more than sixty enzyme reactions involving key elements of body chemistry including hormone production and nerve conduction. Deficiency causes anemia, weakness, possible urinary stones.

Found In: Liver, fish, brown rice, most vegetables, some fruits such as bananas and grapes. Vitamin B6 is also found in lean meats, fish, butter, eggs, cheese, and milk. Easily destroyed in milling of cereals, and cooking of foods from animal sources.

How Much Do We Need? About 2.5 mg per day. In doses of up to 10 mg a day, it can help prevent kidney stones, but in larger doses can be toxic.

Vitamin B12 (Cobalamin)

Functions: Prevention of pernicious anemia. Acts as a crucial component in chemical enzyme reaction for nerve conduction, and synthesis of DNA within the cells.

Found In: Foods of animal origin only. Meats, egg yolks, fish, cheese, and milk contain vitamin B12. There is none in fruit, vegetables, or grains. Thus strict vegetarians may very well need a supplement.

How Much Do We Need? Approximately 6 micrograms per day. If a key element called *intrinsic factor* is missing in the stomach lining, B12 cannot be absorbed at all by mouth. Pernicious anemia will result unless injections can be given. In all other cases, routine injections of B12 are a waste of time and money.

Folic Acid

Functions: Essential for five different enzyme systems including red blood cell production and nervous system. Helps prevent anemia.

Found In: Liver, wheat bran, spinach, beans, grains. Lesser amounts are found in lean meats, dairy products, and most fresh fruits and vegetables.

How Much Do We Need? Approximately .4 mg per day.

Biotin

Functions: Maintenance of normal nervous tissue, good growth, and so on. Deficiency causes lethargy, depression, sensitivity to touch or pain, and high cholesterol in the blood, along with ECG changes.

Found In: Eggs, cheese, soybeans, meats, cereals, fruits, and vegetables.

How Much Do We Need? 0.2 mg per day.

Pantothenic Acid

Functions: Part of the enzyme metabolism for regulating energy. Helps prevent impairment of defenses against infection, fatigue, and so on.

Found In: Eggs, meats, wheat bran, peanuts, broccoli, cauliflower, cabbage.

How Much Do We Need? Approximately 10 mg per day. There is no toxicity from overdose for humans.

Vitamin C

Functions Prevention of scurvy, which used to be widespread, causing illness or death in up to 90 percent of a ship's crew within a couple of months at sea. Vitamin C is essential in a host of chemical reactions within the body, and is needed for creating hormones, healing wounds, keeping cholesterol balanced, and aiding absorption of iron into the bloodstream from the stomach. Commonly used as a supplement in cases of urinary tract infection, to acidify the urine.

Found In: Surprisingly, the greatest amounts are found in black currants, sweet peppers, broccoli, and Brussels sprouts. It is in much greater quantities in these foods than in citrus fruits. In the North American diet, tomatoes are the number one source of vitamin C, because of their high consumption (about 70 pounds per person per year). Citrus fruits do contain medium amounts of vitamin C. Vitamin C is relatively fragile, and can be destroyed to some extent by overcooking.

How Much Do We Need? In terms of scurvy prevention, the basic requirement is only 60 mg a day. However, Dr. Linus Pauling has suggested that doses up to 2,300 mg are helpful for prevention of colds.

There is considerable scientific debate on this particular point, but it is well known that doses of 1,000 mg are taken without any harmful side effects in adults.

Tremendous claims are made for megadoses of vitamins. These include: longer life, increased sexual potency, decreased cancer, and decreased heart disease. Such claims are basically unfounded. Self-medication with vitamins can produce serious and even fatal side effects. It is obvious that self-diagnosis and treatment with vitamins alone for such conditions as cancer is a tragic mistake. No amount of vitamin therapy can replace close consultations with your physician in cases of known disease.

However, there has been enough research to show that vitamins C and E can both be depleted during times of stress. Both have also been suggested as helpful in the prevention of cancer of the colon. Thus it seems reasonable to include modest amounts of each in your daily supplement.

Minerals

Calcium

Functions: Formation of bones, maintenance of cell structures, blood clotting.

Found In: Milk products, soups or stews that have parts of the bone left during cooking, gelatin powders, nuts, legumes, some other vegetables.

How Much Do We Need? 800 mg per day.

Potassium

Functions: Muscle metabolism, especially cardiac muscle; nerve tissues.

Found In: Meats, dairy products, bananas, overripe tomatoes.

How Much Do We Need? Supplements not needed unless recommended by doctor; for example, when on diuretic therapy.

Zinc

Functions: Essential for over seventy enzyme systems, including synthesis of key protein for growth, sexual maturation, wound healing, maintenance of skin, hair, nails. Deficiency may be seen in cases of acute and chronic stress (where the increased production of corticoids increases its excretion in urine, and decreases blood levels). Deficiency may also be seen in athletes during periods of high exertion, and some cases of very high fiber diet, which binds zinc and prevents it from being absorbed. Deficiencies of zinc cause a low sperm count, poor appetite, weakening of the white blood cells' ability to fight infection, dermatitis, diarrhea, loss of hair, and poor wound healing.

Lack of zinc can also interfere with vitamin A metabolism. Thus, deficiency can cause night blindness. Loss of the senses of taste and smell are also reported. Zinc deficiencies have now been recognized to occur mainly in children who eat little or no meat and dairy products. Strict vegetarians may also be at risk because of the poor absorbability of zinc from the intestines in the presence of cereal grains.

Zinc samples tested by hair analysis are not accurate, because zinc levels in one part of the body do not necessarily reflect what is going on in another part. The results are usually unreliable. I strongly suggest you do not waste your money on such tests. To approach an accurate figure for zinc status in the body, one needs levels from properly sampled hair (new growth), along with blood serum, red blood cells, and for men, semen.

Zinc deficiency has been shown to cause a poor rate of growth in children. This is quite correctable with a zinc supplement.

Found In: Meat, eggs, seafoods—especially oysters (which perhaps gives some substance to the legend that oysters have aphrodisiac powers). Lesser amounts of zinc are also found in milk and dairy products. Excesses of zinc, for example, 150 mg per day, can become your enemy, causing copper deficiency that results in anemia.

One reason for zinc's continued attraction to researchers in the field of infertility is that zinc is found in the greatest concentration in the prostate gland. Some infertility cases associated with low zinc in the semen respond very well to zinc therapy, with many cures reported. In the trade, this benefit is colloquially referred to as "zinc for the dink."

In fact, impotence caused by a severe zinc deficiency can be completely corrected by zinc therapy. However, this type of impotence is quite rare. A full investigation of the condition by your doctor is warranted before taking any

home remedies. It is important to remember
that high doses of zinc may cause a lower blood
copper level. Blood cholesterol and triglyc-
erides may also rise. These are certainly most
undesirable side effects of excesses of this
mineral. Huge doses, such as 6,000 mg, are
usually fatal.

How Much Do We Need? 20 mg per day.

Copper

Functions: Aids utilization of iron; helps
prevent anemia. Useful when taking zinc, to
aid in the absorption of this mineral.

Found In: Liver, shellfish, nuts, and beans. Up
to half your daily requirements can also come
from your water supply system, if you have
copper piping. Deficiencies of copper are
extremely rare.

How Much Do We Need? 2 mg per day.

Iron

Functions: The key element of hemoglobin,
the compound in your blood cells that carries
oxygen to the tissues. Iron is also found in
muscle tissue. With iron deficiency, anemia
quickly follows. Symptoms include fatigue,
pallor, shortness of breath on exercise.

Found In: Virtually any organism that has a
blood supply, such as meats, fowl, fish. Also
found in beans and peas, enriched grains,
shellfish, dried fruits. Iron absorption can be
interfered with by high doses of zinc. Vitamin

C can enhance this absorption, although vitamin C reduces the absorption of copper. (As you can see, figuring out the doses that are appropriate for you to take is not a job for the home hobbyist!)

How Much Do We Need? Approximately 20 mg per day for menstruating women, and 10 mg for men. These figures are based on the fact that only about 10 percent of the iron will be absorbed. Pregnant and lactating women need more (consult your doctor). Vegetarians must be particularly careful because vegetable iron is much more difficult to absorb than iron from animal sources.

In cases of continued iron deficiency in spite of taking adequate supplements, it is important that your doctor find out the reason. A chronic low blood loss from a precancerous polyp in the bowel is one of the most frequent causes. Detected early, such lesions are usually harmless. If not detected at all, they can go on to become fatal. One of the important tests done by your physical examination will be a test for occult, or "hidden," blood in your stools.

It is important *not* to take iron unless you consult your physician, as it can be an extremely dangerous supplement. I have seen one case of death in a two-year-old child from as few as eight tablets of his mother's iron supplement. Even after the child's stomach was pumped out, the amount of iron ingested went on to cause death after only a few days in the hospital.

A Note on Amino Acids

There are twenty-two kinds of amino acids in the body. Nine of these are essential (in other words, must be consumed in your daily diet). The sequence of amino acids in chain (or ladder) formation determines the type of protein. All nine of the essential amino acids are equally important. But only three are likely to be deficient in most diets—lysine, tryptophan, and methionine. All can be found in a vegetarian diet, as well as in meat. Meat does not have any "special kinds" of protein. Remember that it is important to have a variety of foods. No one food has sufficient quantities of all the essential amino acids.

For example, beans, peas, and other vegetables tend to be high in lysine and tryptophan, but low in methionine. Rice and other grains are low in lysine and high in methionine. Thus a meal of beans and rice would tend to give you complete protein. However, there is really no need to do such in-depth analysis of your food. Simply have something from each of the four food groups in your diet every day. Protein requirements increase during pregnancy, during the growth years of childhood, in post-burn or surgical cases, and during the weight gain phase in body building.

Appendix C

Calorie and Fiber Chart

When you have read this chart, you will see how easy it is to make food choices that greatly increase your intake of calories, yet leave you feeling unsatisfied. This is the calorie count for a typical fast-food meal:

Hamburger	470
French fries (20)	310
Large cola (12 oz.)	154
Ice cream cone (1 scoop)	174
TOTAL	1,108 calories

As you can see, this meal adds up to most of the calories that the diet-conscious person should eat in one day, let alone in one meal! And, because the meal is very low in fiber as well, all of those calories still leave you feeling hungry a few hours later.

Use this chart to choose foods that are consistent with our program of a diet balanced in all six food categories. (See Chapter 5.) Relatively good "bargain" foods that provide high fiber are in bold-face type.

Food	Portion	Calories	Dietary Fiber (grams)
Apple	**1 medium**	**70**	**4**
Apple pie	1 piece	300	2.7
Applesauce, sweetened	½ cup	120	2.7
unsweetened	½ cup	55	2.7
Asparagus	**½ cup**	**17**	**1.7**
Avocado	½ medium	170	2.8
Banana	**1 medium**	**100**	**3**
Beans, baked, canned	**½ cup**	**90**	**8**
black	**½ cup**	**95**	**9.7**
green	**½ cup**	**10**	**2.1**
kidney	**½ cup**	**94**	**9.7**
lima	**½ cup**	**118**	**3.7**
navy	**½ cup**	**80**	**8**
pinto	**½ cup**	**78**	**9.4**
white	**½ cup**	**80**	**8**
Bean sprouts (mung)	**¼ cup**	**7**	**0.8**
Beef, rib roast	4 oz.	320	—
steak	4 oz.	422	—
Blackberries, raw	**½ cup**	**27**	**4.4**
Bologna	1 slice	130	—
Brazil nuts	**2 nuts**	**48**	**2.5**
Bread, cracked wheat	2 slices	120	3.6
high bran	**2 slices**	**150**	**7.0**
rye (whole grain)	**2 slices**	**108**	**5.8**
white	2 slices	160	1.9
whole wheat	**2 slices**	**140**	**6.5**
Broccoli	**½ cup**	**15**	**4**

Food	Portion	Calories	Dietary Fiber (grams)
Brussels sprouts	**½ cup**	**24**	**3**
Bulgur, soaked or cooked	**1 cup**	**160**	**9.6**
Butter	1 tsp.	36	—
	1 tbsp.	100	—
Cabbage, cooked	**½ cup**	**11**	**2.8**
raw	**½ cup**	**8**	**1.5**
Cantaloupe	¼ medium	38	1
Carrots	**½ cup**	**20**	**3.4**
Cauliflower	**½ cup**	**12**	**1.8**
Celery	**½ cup**	**10**	**4**
Cereal, All-Bran	**⅓ cup**	**70**	**9**
Bran Buds	**⅓ cup**	**70**	**8**
Bran Chex	⅔ cup	90	6.4
Bran Flakes	⅔ cup	90	4
Bran Muffin Crisp	⅔ cup	130	4
Cracklin' Oat Bran	½ cup	120	4
Fiber One	**½ cup**	**60**	**12**
Fruit & Fibre	½ cup	90	4
Fruitful Bran	¾ cup	120	4
Nabisco 100% Bran	**½ cup**	**70**	**9**
Natural Bran Flakes	⅔ cup	90	5
Puffed Wheat	1 cup	43	3.3
Quaker Oats (long cooking)	1 ounce	110	0.3
Raisin Bran	¾ cup	110	4
Total	1 cup	110	2
Wheaties	1 ounce	110	2

Food	Portion	Calories	Dietary Fiber (grams)
Cheese, Cheddar, Swiss, or Parmesan, grated	1 tbsp.	28	—
Cottage	½ cup	48	—
Cherries, sweet, raw	10	38	1.2
canned in light syrup	½ cup	55	1
Chestnuts, roasted	**2 large**	**29**	**1.9**
Chicken, dark meat, no skin	4 oz.	112	—
dark meat with skin, fried	4 oz.	300	—
White meat, no skin	4 oz.	104	—
white meat, with skin, fried	4 oz.	262	—
Chickpeas	**½ cup**	**86**	**6**
Coconut, dried, sweetened	1 tbsp.	46	3.4
unsweetened	1 tbsp.	22	3.4
Cookies, chocolate chip	2 large	240	—
Fibermed® high fiber cookies	**2**	**120**	**10**
Corn, sweet, on cob	**1 medium**	**70**	**5**
kernels, canned	**½ cup**	**64**	**5**
Cornbread	**2½-in. sq.**	**93**	**3.4**
Crackers, graham	2	54	1.4
Ry-Krisp	2	42	1.5
soda (saltine)	2	26	0.2
Triscuit	**2**	**50**	**2**
Wheat Thins	**6**	**58**	**2.2**
Cucumber, raw, unpeeled	10 slices	12	0.7
Dates	**2**	**39**	**1.2**

Food	Portion	Calories	Dietary Fiber (grams)
Eggplant	**½ cup**	**17**	**1.5**
Egg, boiled	1	80	—
fried (1 tsp. fat)	1	108	—
Figs, dried	**3**	**120**	**10.5**
fresh	**1**	**30**	**2**
Fish, cod	4 oz.	86	—
flounder	4 oz.	86	—
halibut	4 oz.	100	—
salmon	4 oz.	240	—
sardines, canned	4 oz.	160	—
sole	4 oz.	86	—
tuna (water pack)	¼ cup	50	—
Grapefruit	½ medium	30	0.8
Grapes, green	20	75	1
red or black	20	65	1
Gravy, brown, meat	2 tbsp.	82	—
Greens, cooked **(collard, beet, chard, kale)**	**½ cup**	**20**	**4**
Ham, lean	2 slices	75	—
Hamburger, meat only	4 oz.	180	—
with bun		400	1.9
Hot dog, beef, meat only	1	125	—
with bun	1	262	1.9
Honeydew melon	¼ medium	42	1.5
Lamb, lean	4 oz.	200	—
Lentils, brown, cooked	**½ cup**	**108**	**4.1**
red, cooked	**½ cup**	**96**	**3.2**

Food	Portion	Calories	Dietary Fiber (grams)
Lettuce, shredded	**1 cup**	**5**	**0.8**
Macaroni and cheese, baked	1 cup	497	2.0
Macaroni, whole wheat	**1 cup**	**200**	**5.7**
Margarine	1 tbsp.	100	—
Milk buttermilk	1 cup	80	—
homogenized	1 cup	161	—
skim	1 cup	84	—
2%	1 cup	130	—
Milk Products cream, whipping	1 cup	869	—
cream, table	1 cup	493	—
ice cream	1 scoop	174	—
ice milk	1 scoop	137	—
sour cream	1 cup	328	—
yogurt (low fat)	1 cup	128	—
Muffins, bran, no raisins or dates	**1**	**78**	**2.3**
English, whole wheat	**1**	**125**	**3.7**
homemade, bran, whole wheat	**1**	**68**	**2.3**
Mushrooms, raw	**4**	**4**	**1.4**
sautéed	4	45	1.4
Noodles, egg	**½ cup**	**98**	**3.0**
whole wheat egg	**1 cup**	**200**	**5.7**
Olives, green or black	6	42	1.2
Onions, cooked	**½ cup**	**22**	**1.5**
green	**½ cup**	**22**	**1.6**

Food	Portion	Calories	Dietary Fiber (grams)
Orange	1	**70**	**2.4**
Peach, canned in syrup	2 halves	70	1.4
raw	1	38	2.3
Peanut butter	1 tbsp.	86	1.1
Peanuts, dry roasted	**10**	**100**	**2.2**
Peas, black-eyed	**½ cup**	**74**	**8**
green	**½ cup**	**60**	**9.1**
split	**½ cup**	**63**	**6.7**
peas and carrots, frozen	**5 oz.**	**40**	**6.2**
Pear, raw	**1 medium**	**70**	**2.4**
Pepper, green	**2 tbsp.**	**4**	**0.3**
Pineapple, canned	½ cup	74	0.8
fresh	½ cup	41	0.8
Plums	**2**	**38**	**2**
Popcorn (no oil or butter added)	**1 cup**	**20**	**1**
Pork, bacon	3 slices	120	—
boneless, lean	4 oz.	242	—
Potatoes, baked in skin	**1 medium**	**91**	**5**
boiled in skin	**1 medium**	**80**	**3.5**
French fried	10 pieces	155	3
mashed	**½ cup**	**85**	**3**
sweet, baked or boiled	**1 small**	**146**	**4**
Prunes	3	122	1.9
Raisins, seedless	1 tbsp.	29	1
Raspberries	**½ cup**	**20**	**4.6**
Rhubarb, cooked with sugar	½ cup	169	2.9

Food	Portion	Calories	Dietary Fiber (grams)
Rice, brown	**½ cup**	**83**	**5.5**
instant	½ cup	79	0.7
white	½ cup	79	2.1
Rutabaga (yellow turnip)	**½ cup**	**40**	**3.2**
Salad oil	1 tbsp.	100	—
Salami	1 slice	130	—
Sauerkraut (canned)	**⅔ cup**	**15**	**3.1**
Seafood			
Clams, canned	½ cup	52	—
crabmeat	½ cup	84	—
scallops	½ cup	160	—
shrimp	½ cup	91	—
Soft drinks			
Club soda	6 oz.	0	—
Cola	6 oz.	72	—
Orange	6 oz.	82	—
Root beer	6 oz.	82	—
7-Up	6 oz.	72	—
Tonic water	6 oz.	54	—
Spaghetti, whole wheat	**1 cup**	**200**	**5.6**
Spinach, raw	**1 cup**	**8**	**3.5**
cooked	**½ cup**	**26**	**7**
Squash, summer	**½ cup**	**8**	**2**
winter	**½ cup**	**50**	**3.5**
zucchini	**½ cup**	**7**	**3**
Strawberries, raw, no sugar	**1 cup**	**45**	**3**

Food	Portion	Calories	Dietary Fiber (grams)
Tomato, catsup	1 tbsp.	18	0.2
sauce	½ cup	20	0.5
Tomatoes, canned	½ cup	21	1
raw	**1 small**	**22**	**1.4**
Tortillas	2 6-inch	140	4
Turkey, roasted	1 slice	80	—
Walnuts, chopped	1 tbsp.	49	1.1
Watermelon	**1 slice**	**68**	**2.8**
Yams, cooked or baked in skin	**1 medium**	**156**	**6.8**

SECOND WEEK:	TOTAL CALORIES CONSUMED (SEE FIGURE 7.2 OR APPENDIX C)		TOTAL CALORIES BURNED OFF (SEE FIGURE 7.1)	
Day 1		cal.		cal.
Day 2		cal.		cal.
Day 3		cal.		cal.
Day 4		cal.		cal.
Day 5		cal.		cal.
Day 6		cal.		cal.
Day 7		cal.		cal.

Sub-total   cal.   Sub-total   cal.

÷ 7 =   Calorie intake per day   ÷ 7 =   Calorie burn-off per day

CALORIE INTAKE   ▢ — ▢ = ▢

Average calories consumed per day   Average calories burned off per day   Average net calories intake per day

WEIGHT CHANGE   ▢ — ▢ = ▢

Starting weight on Day 1   Weight after second week   Weight change in one week

THIRD WEEK:	TOTAL CALORIES CONSUMED (SEE FIGURE 7.2 OR APPENDIX C)		TOTAL CALORIES BURNED OFF (SEE FIGURE 7.1)
Day 1		cal.	cal.
Day 2		cal.	cal.
Day 3		cal.	cal.
Day 4		cal.	cal.
Day 5		cal.	cal.
Day 6		cal.	cal.
Day 7		cal.	cal.

Sub-total ____ cal.   Sub-total ____ cal.

÷ 7 = ____ Calorie intake per day   ÷ 7 = ____ Calorie burn-off per day

CALORIE INTAKE ____ — ____ = ____

Average calories consumed per day   Average calories burned off per day   Average net calories intake per day

WEIGHT CHANGE ____ — ____ = ____

Starting weight on Day 1   Weight after third week   Weight change in one week

FOURTH WEEK: **TOTAL CALORIES CONSUMED (SEE FIGURE 7.2 OR APPENDIX C)**   **TOTAL CALORIES BURNED OFF (SEE FIGURE 7.1)**

Day 1	cal.	cal.
Day 2	cal.	cal.
Day 3	cal.	cal.
Day 4	cal.	cal.
Day 5	cal.	cal.
Day 6	cal.	cal.
Day 7	cal.	cal.

Sub-total [ ] cal.   Sub-total [ ] cal.

÷ 7 = [ ] Calorie intake per day   ÷ 7 = [ ] Calorie burn-off per day

CALORIE INTAKE [ ] **—** [ ] **=** [ ]

Average calories consumed per day   Average calories burned off per day   Average net calories intake per day

WEIGHT CHANGE [ ] **—** [ ] **=** [ ]

Starting weight on Day 1   Weight after fourth week   Weight change in one week

266

FIFTH WEEK:	TOTAL CALORIES CONSUMED (SEE FIGURE 7.2 OR APPENDIX C)		TOTAL CALORIES BURNED OFF (SEE FIGURE 7.1)	
Day 1		cal.		cal.
Day 2		cal.		cal.
Day 3		cal.		cal.
Day 4		cal.		cal.
Day 5		cal.		cal.
Day 6		cal.		cal.
Day 7		cal.		cal.

Sub-total [ ] cal.   ÷ 7 = [ ] Calorie intake per day

Sub-total [ ] cal.   ÷ 7 = [ ] Calorie burn-off per day

CALORIE INTAKE

[ ] — [ ] = [ ]

Average calories consumed per day

Average calories burned off per day

Average net calories intake per day

WEIGHT CHANGE

[ ] — [ ] = [ ]

Starting weight on Day 1

Weight after fifth week

Weight change in one week

Appendix D

Examples of a Balanced Diet

As discussed in Chapter 5, the elements of a good balanced diet can be divided into the following six categories:
1. Protein.
2. Fats.
3. Carbohydrates.
4. Fiber.
5. Vitamins and Minerals.
6. Water.

In choosing foods to ensure that you obtain enough of these elements in your diet, it is helpful to keep the four basic food groups in mind:
1. Milk Group.
2. Meat Group.
3. Vegetable-Fruit Group.
4. Bread-Cereal Group.

Generally speaking, choosing some foods from each food group is the easiest way to make sure your diet is balanced. The following are some sample meals based on this principle. (Of course, if you are a vegetarian or have other special dietary considerations, you may need to make some adjustments to these menus.)

Sample Balanced Breakfasts

1. Milk, whole-grain cereal, scrambled eggs and toast, orange.
2. Cheese, cold sliced meat, rye bread, half grapefruit.

Sample Balanced Lunches

1. Tuna salad with lettuce and tomato, whole wheat toast, ice cream.
2. Vegetable beef soup, whole wheat crackers, cottage cheese with fresh fruit.

Sample Balanced Dinners

1. Roast chicken, baked potato, tossed salad, dinner roll, pudding made with milk.
2. Lamp chop, boiled brown rice, green peas, carrot sticks, sherbet.

Bibliography and Recommended Reading

Comfort, Alex. *The Joy of Sex.* New York: Simon & Schuster, 1974.

Cousins, Norman. *Anatomy of an Illness as Perceived by the Patient.* New York: Bantam, 1981.

Eyton, Audrey. *The F-Plan Diet.* New York: Bantam, 1982.

Friedman, Meyer, and Rosenman, Ray H. *Type A Behavior and Your Heart.* New York: Fawcett, 1981.

Johnson, Spencer, and Blanchard, Kenneth. *The One Minute Manager.* New York: Morrow, 1982.

Mandino, Og. *The Choice.* New York: Bantam, 1984.

Masters, William H., and Johnson, Virginia E. *Human Sexual Inadequacy.* New York: Bantam, 1980.

Peale, Norman Vincent. *The Power of Positive Thinking.* Old Tappan, New Jersey: Revell, 1966.

Peter, Laurence, and Hull, Raymond. *The Peter Principle: Why Things Always Go Wrong.* New York: Morrow, 1969.

Selye, Hans. *The Stress of Life.* New York: McGraw-Hill, 1956.

Selye, Hans. *Stress without Distress.* New York: Lippincott, 1974.

Tanner, Ogden et al. *Human Behaviour: Stress.* New York: Time-Life, 1976

Wilson, Larry, and Johnson, Spencer. *The One Minute Sales Person.* New York: Morrow, 1984.

Index

Peter G. Hanson, M.D.

Dr. Peter Hanson has enthralled audiences of all ages and backgrounds throughout Canada, the United States, and Europe with his direct, often humorous approach to personal stress management.

Born in Vancouver, British Columbia, in 1947, Peter Hanson lived in five of Canada's ten provinces while growing up, and his qualities as a public speaker began to surface early. By age 14, he was working in live television production as a studio director — as well as performing on-camera comedy monologues.

But despite his comedic talents, Dr. Hanson had serious career objectives. At the age of 23, he graduated from the University of Toronto Medical School. One year later he was appointed team doctor for the Toronto Argonaut Football Club — North America's youngest physician to hold the position of team doctor with a major professional sports organization.

Further establishing his medical credentials, Dr. Hanson was involved for three years in the busy emergency department of a suburban Toronto hospital. In 1973 he established an office practice that grew to include more than 4,000 active patients, from new borns to centenarians.

Dr. Hanson's medical practice has been the subject of a number of articles in medical journal's and has been called one of the most innovative and well-run family practices on the continent.

innovative and well-run family practices on the continent. Surprisingly, he still does house calls.

One measure of the respect he has gained in the Canadian medical community is that Dr. Hanson has lectured to other doctors on practice management and office reorganization.

Dr. Hanson is available for speaking engagements and seminars. In the United States, contact:

National Speakers Bureau
222 Wisconsin Avenue
Lake Forest, Illinois 60045
(800) 323-9442 or (708) 295-1122

In Canada, contact:

1-800-665-7376

Dr. Hanson would also be pleased to hear from his readers. If you have a question or comment, please write directly to:

Dr. Peter Hanson
Hanson Stress International
% R & R Book Bar
14800 Yonge Street
Aurora, Ontario, Canada
L4G 1N3
(416) 232-0687

Due to volume Dr. Hanson may not be able to answer all letters personally.

NEW! "Power Nap" tape... available by mail!

This new audiocassette — "The Joy of Stress *Power Nap*" — demonstrates Dr. Peter G. Hanson's unique techniques for taking quick, energizing, stress-relieving naps throughout your day. Not a reading from the book, "Power Nap" was researched, written and recorded by Dr. Hanson. This tape is available in many bookstores or by ordering from the coupon below. Playing time: 60 minutes.

Peter G. Hanson, M.D.

STRESS for SUCCESS

Thriving On Stress At Work

From the author of the international bestseller
THE JOY OF STRESS
Over 1/2 million copies sold

Order your copy now: $22.95 (plus $2.50 handling)
R & R Book Bar, 14800 Yonge St. Aurora, Ont. L4G 1N3